Honesty Victimised

CBI POLITICISED

Honesty Victimised

CBI POLITICISED

Rear Admiral BR Menon (Retd) VSM

Manas Publications
(We Convert Fighters into Writers)
New Delhi - 110 002 (INDIA)

MANAS PUBLICATIONS
(We Convert Fighters into Writers)
(Publishers, Library Suppliers, Importers & Exporters)
4402/5-A, Ansari Road (Opp. HDFC Bank)
Darya Ganj, New Delhi - 110 002 (India)
Phones: Off.: 011-23260783, 23265523, Res.: 011-23842660
E-mail: manaspublications@gmail.com
manaspublications@yahoo.com
Website: www.manaspublications.in

ISBN 978-81-7049-548-2
₹ 695

Designed by
Veronica Grafic Arts

Printed in India at
R.K. Print Services, Delhi

Published by Mrs Suman Lata for
Manas Publications
4402/5-A, Ansari Road (Opp HDFC Bank),
Darya Ganj, New Delhi - 110002 (INDIA)

To

my wife

GIRIJA (PROMILA)

whose immense patience, forbearance, courage of conviction, spiritual strength of mind and unfathomable ability to forgive the sins of others alone made it possible for me to dig my heel in and face the consequences of the onslaught of political VICTIMISATION when battled against HONESTY. It is SHE who emboldened me to fight to the finish.

Foreword

I have known Admiral Menon for more than forty years. Heralded in the Indian Navy as a dynamic and outstanding Professional Officer, ever in pursuit of excellence, his contribution has been profound and unique in whatever field he was entrusted with. Erudite in Marine Engineering, being one of the few officers trained in Royal Naval Engineering College at Greenwich, UK, Ravi as popularly known amongst his peer group steered the growth of the Marine Engineering in the Indian Navy in its multi-dimensional facets, taking a perspicacious view in tandem with the technology, with a visionary approach. With stellar leadership qualities coupled with a high ethic and value system, he has always been the epitome of a great personality. We had served together as Diplomats at the Indian High Commission in the UK in early '80s, where I witnessed his remarkable diplomatic skills in advancing the Indo-UK cooperation.

He rose quickly up the ladder to become a Flag Officer in the Indian Navy. He then got disenchanted with the Navy, when it was felt that certain exclusive perks and privileges – including the post of Chief of Naval Staff – were denied to the Technical Officers, which led to his frustration and eventual resignation from the service in 1994, as portrayed in this book very vividly. Admiral Menon thereafter became the head honcho of the Goa Shipyard Ltd (GSL), especially chosen by the Defence Ministry and Navy, to bolster the productivity of the GSL to meet the exacting requirements of the Navy. Little did he realize then that it would be a watershed moment in his career with travails and tribulations to follow.

As I know, Ravi always liked to fish in troubled waters and without exceptions, took the road less travelled by accepting the challenges all the way with indomitable spirit. GSL was perhaps the ideal ground for him to accept the new challenges with inherent risks involved, to steer to become the numero uno organisation. He did it, but at great cost to his personal life. His tryst with GSL began when he met with huge resistance from the Union leaders from within and outside, for attempting to bring in industrial discipline and professionalism into the workforce to improve productivity. The trouble mounted when CISF (Central Industrial Security Force) was inducted for the first time in the GSL to maintain discipline and ensure overall security of the Yard, an unprecedented move which was attempted by many of the previous CMDs but to no avail. The Unions were disparaging the CMD's achievements, since it was not to their advantage at all. Trouble mounted for Admiral Menon when the political pressure was brought in from both the State and Central level by the Union. Undeterred and unabashed, he continued with a slew of productive and welfare measures which saw the GSL making a quantum jump, including receipt of a foreign order. He need not have rocked the boat and earned the wrath and hostility all around. Maintaining *status quo ante* in the Shipyard would have been a comfort zone to the CMD; but he as a leader with indomitable spirit drove with a visionary club aiming for a hole in one circumventing the hurdles all the way.

The book unravels how the CBI was brought in by the political factions without any basis alleging corruption and accumulation of wealth disproportionate to his known sources of income. The ordeal then began for Ravi; but he stuck to his principle-centred leadership. His house, office and close relatives houses were raided and bank accounts frozen by the CBI without any substantial charge sheet. He, well after retirement in 2000, filed a case against the CBI to release his frozen bank accounts, before even a charge sheet was framed against him; a move that was totally unprecedented. The CBI then – to save their skin – slapped a disproportionate assets case against him. The case went on for the next 12 years onto his retirement proving to the court his income, assets and expenditure. Ironically, the CBI reportedly questioned the account status while he was in the naval service also; whereas he was given Vigilance Clearance four years ago by the same CBI for the post of CMD, GSL.

Ravi was finally acquitted. It was his sheer tenacity, sincerity of purpose, courage of conviction, perseverance and persuasive approach to fight against the system, which got him exonerated. When one is normally reticent to voice the ignominy subjected to, ostracized by the society, Ravi has ventured out boldly in this book to capture every moment of agony and anguish undergone and how he endured it and fought a bitter legal battle for over 12 years to prove his righteousness. Despite persecution and prosecution, it was due to Admiral Menon's strong willpower and assiduousness, the onslaught of CBI could be successively thwarted. Anyone else would have cracked. The fact that even during the pendency of the court case against the CBI, Ravi had served as CMD in PSUs in Kerala and also as Advisor to the Chief Minister of Kerala, bears ample testimony to his utmost integrity and probity in public life.

The book chronicles the entire sequence of events in minutest details and how the trepidation did not deter him fighting against a mighty system, even after post-retirement. It brings to fore a rudimentary and yet an important facet – how one should keep an account of each and every penny of income and expenditure. Who knows – how and when one would be accosted with? GSL has grown manifold over the years; thanks to the strong foundation laid by Ravi. His far-sightedness in inducting the CISF with the Central Government support has paid rich dividends; which ironically was the *raison d'être* for all the untold sufferings. Turning around GSL from an indisciplined Shipyard to one of the best in the country was the singular achievement of Admiral Menon with a patriotic zeal.

Back from Goa to Kerala, a similar fate awaited him when as the Advisor to the Chief Minister of Kerala, he tried to enforce sincerity of purpose and professional ethics in developing Inland Waterways of Kerala by side-lining the corrupt contractors and supporting bureaucracy. The Inland Waterways improved vastly but here again he became a victim of the selfish political factions of the State who were not able to accept his unwavering selfless attitude and boldness of action. As a result he was trapped in a case and was removed from the post of Advisor to the CM. Like the phoenix out of the ashes, he got himself acquitted from the trumpeted case against him in the High Court at the first hearing itself. The Chief Minister was only too keen to re-instate him as his Advisor.

> "Sometimes you have to burn yourself to the ground before you can rise like a phoenix from the ashes." – Jens Lekman

Ravi's case bears ample testimony to it. It is said that Justice and Truth will finally prevail. But at what cost? It is a question of time. By any standards twelve years is indeed a long period and that too for an honest Naval Officer with an impeccable track record all along.

This book will be of great interest to everyone who keeps honesty of purpose and patriotism on their sleeve.

Rear Admiral V Balachandran (Retd)
AVSM, NM, VSM

Rear Admiral Balachandran retired from the Indian Navy in 2007. During the long service spanning over 36 years, he held many important assignments – Assistant Naval Advisor, High Commission of India, London; Commanding Officer, INS Valsura – at Jamnagar, the only high-tech Electrical and Electronics training establishment of the Indian Navy, Commandant of College of Defence Management, Hyderabad and Admiral Superintendent, Naval Dockyard, Mumbai.

What they say ...

Padma Bhushan Sri Vinod Rai, IAS (Retd)

Former Comptroller and Auditor General of India; Secretary, Department of Financial Services, Ministry of Finance, Government of India; Principal Secretary (Finance), Government of Kerala

I am delighted to write a review of the book written by Admiral (Retd) BR Menon. I had known Admiral while I served in the Ministry of Defence in the Government of India and later while I moved to the Government of Kerala. Admiral Menon (Retd) was known as an upright, capable and dynamic officer who led from the front.

It is indeed laudable that Admiral Menon took the decision to write this book. I am sure it will give him the satisfaction to chronicle the travails of being the lone crusader against a system which is well entrenched as a parasite on public institutions and a constant black mark on every aspect of public life. More importantly, it will serve as a beacon to those placed in similar predicaments, and often, at the mercy of those very persons who are assigned to protect them. The book is a remarkable saga of the challenges and perils of being in public service. It is the story of how, while in the short run, the corrupt, misguided and crooked emerge as the winners, in the long run it is always the victory of the honest over the vile. It is only a question of retaining one's equanimity and tenacity. The book is a very detailed and objective account of how vested interests try insidious means to ensure that their stranglehold on an organisation remains intact for them to pursue their nefarious activities. However, to be able to withstand the onslaught of such vested interests, one requires enormous amount of courage of conviction and steadfast commitment to probity and ethics in public life.

The book also gives a very important message. The CBI is the country's premier investigating agency. There are competing demands on its manpower resources. There is thus need for it to prioritise its scarce capabilities and concentrate on the 'big fish' rather than thinly deploy these resources over a whole gamut of trumped up cases which prove nothing in the end but merely serve to demotivate sincere and honest public officials. It also brings out the need for the agency to separate the wheat from the chaff and expunge the cases with no content, from its active registers so as to be able to concentrate on the more 'meaty' investigations. The courage to close such inconsequential and motivated cases should be the hallmark of a capable head of the organisation.

Public service is indeed a roadway paved with thorns. An official is expected to serve with dedication and commitment, integrity and honesty and with the spirit of service to the nation. Even if one were to disregard the adverse comparison that obtains vis-a-vis posts of equivalent responsibility in the private sector, the oversight by vigilance agencies is enormous and often very demoralising. Thus, the disproportionately low compensation coupled with 'occupational hazards' is becoming an increasingly major deterrent in attracting capable and qualified youngsters to the public sector. Coupled with these two negatives, is the increasing interference and overpowering influence of a political executive, which has begun to seek executive control over administration itself. To wean administration away from such debilitating influences, certain very critical reforms are necessary. The earlier that these are introduced, the better it will be for sustainable economic development of the country. For such long-term sustainable development, good governance is an important pillar. It is fervently hoped that steps will soon be taken to ensure that the best of talent is attracted to the public sector and the negative influences that overpower, diminish.

This book will go a long way in encouraging bold and honest administrators to maintain their independence as, theirs will be the ultimate victory.

I am sure this book will have a great sales run.

Admiral VS Shekhawat (Retd), PVSM, AVSM, VSM

Former Chief of the Naval Staff, Indian Navy

This short book by Admiral Menon will interest all who have worked in manufacturing industries or have had dealings with public sector enterprises. It will particularly interest those who may have received the unwelcome attentions of the governments' investigative agencies despite no criminal act on their part. It should however be required reading for all young military officers, perhaps all civil servants too, to be better prepared for the challenges and dilemmas lying ahead in their careers and the moral fibre required to face vicious vested interests – political, institutional and personal, and overcome them through self-belief, ingrained sense of duty and responsibility, moral courage, and ultimately faith – in oneself, in the good in others and above all in eventual justice for the righteous.

The gist of the tale is easily told. The author nurses a consuming, gnawing sense of perceived discrimination against technical officers in the Indian Navy, despite having attained high rank but not being eligible for the highest, that of the Chief of the Naval Staff, a post restricted to executive officers who have held specified criteria appointments. When opportunity offers, he seizes it by volunteering to head the Goa Shipyard Ltd (GSL), a public sector enterprise under the Ministry of Defence (MoD) while still remaining in the navy which means so much to him.

In GSL he runs headlong into the entrenched forces of a lethargic, undisciplined, unionized workforce, a collusive security set-up, low productivity and profitability, absence of shipbuilding orders due to poor reputation for quality and delivery and local politicians fishing in troubled waters for influence and votes. As an outstanding naval engineer with a strong sense of duty and discipline, he earnestly sets about enforcing a modicum of responsibility and accountability, soon to discover that he has put his hand into a hornets' nest of corruption and sloth.

It is the beginning of his troubles with the unions, authorities, threats and political pressures, contrived cases in courts, and the turning loose upon him of the coercive powers of the State. It is remarkable that in the face of every kind of malign influence, he continued his dedicated efforts to completely turn around the performance, profitability, reputation and worker morale of GSL whilst ensuring discipline, accountability and harmonious relations. This naturally did not suit the unexpectedly marginalized disruptive forces who had their ill-gotten benefits snatched from them, and who then schemed and connived to somehow dislodge an inconvenient CMD, to the extent of hounding him through a compliant CBI even after his full tenure of five years at GSL, well into his retirement. Despite the support of the officials of the MoD, though not of the then Defence Minister, George Fernandes, who apparently went out of his way to harass the officer for his own ends, it would take him twelve long, wasted years of struggle in courts to completely clear his name.

The start of his second innings after GSL, in Kerala with TELK, Inland Waterways restoration and finally as Advisor to the Chief Minister, was equally disillusioning, but there too he effected a significant turnaround, applying the same methods and upright determination which was the hallmark of his GSL success.

The culminating court judgement acquitting him of all charges bears testimony to the precise and meticulous manner in which he marshalled his defence, and is a searing judicial indictment of misapplied power of the state in coercing upright individuals who place the public good above their own personal convenience, and courageously oppose the machinations of nefarious, corrupt forces.

Perhaps fortuitously, the book is also a tribute to the Indian judicial process, convoluted though it might be, and especially to the lady judge who finally disposed off his case, demolishing the concocted charges against him in a well reasoned, cogent, clear and elegant order.

Vice Admiral IC Rao (Retd), PVSM, AVSM, VSM

Former Chief of Material (Head of Technical Branches), Indian Navy

I have known Ravi Menon since 1973 by which time he had been recognised as an outstanding young Naval Lieutenant and a brilliant engineer. He was selected for further training in engineering design. He learnt about shipbuilding as an overseer at the Garden Reach Shipbuilders and Engineers Ltd, a Defence PSU at Kolkata. He was selected for prime assignments like Deputy Naval Adviser to the Indian High Commission in London, Head of the Naval Ship Repair Yard at Kochi and Director of Marine Engineering at Naval Headquarters in New Delhi. In each appointment, he made a mark and earned his promotions in full measure. I regret that he moved away from shouldering greater responsibility within the Navy where he could steer issues which had irked him.

The Navy's loss became Goa Shipyard's gain. Productivity in shipyards was notoriously bad and his efforts to turn around GSL were laudable. Heads of Public Sector Units have financial and administrative powers akin to a private company and hence they come under intense pressure from politicians and bureaucrats for undue favours, and they succumb to varying degrees, for sheer survival. Ravi is made of sterner stuff and that is where his troubles arose. His story of how he stood his ground is on the one hand an inspiration to other public sector heads on how to stick to principles one cherishes, and on the other hand, a chilling account of how one has to face the consequences. The stories of how a CBI enquiry is used as a cooked up means to keep opponents in check, in perpetuity, are passé, as long as they refer to others. When it happens to you, it hits home and that is the value of Ravi Menon's book. It is a 'do it yourself guide', on how to do what it takes to overcome the evil machinations of unscrupulous politicians who find pliant policemen to do their bidding without compunction.

I admire the spirit of Ravi and Girija to doggedly pursue their case till final victory. I cannot think of any other couple who would regain their composure after such an ordeal, described to the reader in meticulous detail. Eventually one has to wait for the right person to arrive to get one's due. In Ravi's case it was the Special Judge Anuja Prabhudesai who closed the case. It is a shame that more such accounts are not published by victims of vendettas, and even more shame on our system which takes no action against the perpetrators who act with impunity.

Some people mellow with age but I am happy to say that Ravi is not one of them and this book is testimony that you can't keep a good man down. I recommend a quick read of this book to learn how each one of us has to be prepared to face the consequences, if and when we decide to say NO.

* * *

Padma Bhushan Sri Julio Ribeiro, IPS (Retd)

Former DGP, Maharashtra

Rear Admiral BR Menon (Retd) has sent me the manuscript of a book he intends to publish. The book is about the case registered against him by the CBI when he was the Chairman and Managing Director of Goa Shipyard Ltd, a public sector company, which he headed for 5 years very successfully.

Admiral Menon was prosecuted for possessing assets disproportionate to his known sources of income by the CBI. He proved mathematically that in the period of consideration he had saved about ₹9 lakh by spending less then what he had actually earned. The evidence he produced is mentioned in detail in the judgement of the Session Judge Goa, who tried the case and acquitted the Admiral.

Not knowing Admiral Menon personally, I cannot make a subjective assessment like Admiral Balachandran who wrote the Foreword to the book. I can only go by the contents of the manuscript which confirms my considered opinion that the CBI is no longer an independent investigating authority like it was in its heyday. Steady politicisation has made this premier police investigative agency into a 'caged parrot'. This was sought to be corrected by judicial fiat. It was decided that the Director would be selected by a very high powered triumvirate consisting of the Prime Minister, the leader of the opposition and the Chief Justice of India. Even this arrangement has not succeeded in addressing the problem of political interference in investigations of sensitive cases with political implications.

In this case Admiral Menon alleges that he was hounded by the then Defence Minister George Fernandes, a known trade unionist, because of the pressure put on the Minister by the Trade Union leaders of Goa Shipyard, backed by the local Goa politicians. I am not able to comment on this allegation because I know nothing about it but I can safely say that the investigating officer of the CBI did a very shoddy job by neglecting to inquire into the truth or falsehood of the defence put up by the Admiral in writing. For example, the Admiral has shown that he has earned some amounts of money from the rent paid by tenants for a flat owned by him in Delhi when he was still in the service of the Navy. He had also earned money from breeding and selling Boxer puppies and his wife had worked as an executive in a small company in Delhi when her husband was in the Navy. Even though documentary evidence was produced by the Admiral to prove these sources of income the CBI officer did not check the facts and omitted these earnings from his income. This was inexcusable.

Any investigating agency has to ascertain the truth. They are not supposed to blindly pin down an accused, whether he is guilty or not. When the Admiral had given written statements citing different sources of income it was incumbent on the investigating officer to verify his claim. In this case verification would not involve too much trouble because it was based mainly on documentary evidence and bank account entries. I am not surprised that the Sessions Judge acquitted him honourably.

This brings me to the conclusion of my observations. The CBI is still the preferred vehicle of ascertainment of the truth and it should live up to the expectations of the people. Corruption does enter the equation at times but it is the political pressure applied by politicians in power that the CBI needs to withstand if it is to regain its fading lustre.

* * *

Father Joe Pereira

(Founder, Kripa Foundation, India)

The book *Honesty Victimised – CBI Politicised*, could not have been timed at a better moment than now in our present situation in the country. It was my privilege to get the opportunity of addressing the problem of addiction in the work place for the first time in Goa Shipyard. Admiral Menon was the first to set up an ILO sponsored Workplace Prevention Programme. Together with his beloved wife Girija they reached out to the numerous families of the workers and helped change the quality of life both within the workplace as well as in their neighbourhoods. I was aware of the tremendous strain a man of integrity had to face while he served his country with selflessness and sacrifice. I carried this pain in my heart and I am extremely happy and relieved that Admiral Menon has presented the inside story of his agony.

The minute details of his well-documented transparency is amazing and were it not for the solid base of a strong faith in God he would not have faced this ignominy with such great magnanimity. Behind this one man of integrity stand a whole lot of persecuted persons within a corrupt system of a political choice. Thanks to Admiral Menon for being a voice of the voiceless!

It is time that such revelation help heal our country and prevent more such victimization in times to come corroding the essential fabric of our Noble Nation.

* * *

Author's Point of View

There are numerous instances of innocent government officials who fall prey to CBI enquiries, based on various local inputs from workplace, local vigilance agencies or local political agents to CBI.

To work efficiently and earnestly focusing on a well-crafted path towards a corporate goal, the government officials at times tend to tramp on rules and regulations unknowingly; but that is not always with a view for any financial gains but certainly with an altruistic intention of completing a task – most enthusiastically to the best of his or her ability, on time. They are based on well-meaning intentions – may be bordering on violations of some set rules and regulations perhaps. But the violator is innocent and not guilty of a crime.

Indian laws permit ample scope to analyse and judge a man from his sincere efforts, and resultant achievements – whether he is innocent or not. It is here where our investigating agencies fail miserably. There are a plethora of incidents and examples where CBI have registered cases against individuals based on initial inputs and then more than proving the truth in the case, CBI always tries to prove without exception, that their initial hunch was right and the individual thus chargesheeted is put to unfold misery and punishment, eventually. CBI does not leave any stone unturned in their efforts with all their government machinery at their disposal, to prove that an innocent individual is indeed guilty of the crime he has been chargesheeted for. CBI's 'ego' is at its best then; honesty and truth are given a wide berth or at times all their efforts are to save their skin. CBI's initial chargesheet cannot be wrong – that is their general dictum.

A common government official just cannot defend himself from the onslaught of a well-orchestrated CBI. The innocent defender needs to have huge amount of funds at his disposal which is seldom the case. Most of the time he will be a full time government employee working full time in a government office or in a Corporate sector or in the Defence sector with little time to spare for defending against the might of the CBI. And above all, emotionally he would be a terribly demoralised person in his social and official circle with the print and electronic media having a field day about his case. Within a day of a CBI raid or arrest, the innocent victim gets ostracised from his own friends, relatives, family and society. 90% of the victims simply collapse and lose the will and determination to fight. One has to experience it, to realise its effect on the personality of the victim. I was perhaps one of the few survivors who took a "Never Say Die" attitude, gathered sufficient grit, and fought many legal battles for 13 long years, all alone and eventually won the war against the CBI. I crushed the CBI. The aim of this narrative is two-fold: One, the CBI should realise that they are not just a set of normal Police Constables, Police Officers, and Station-in-Charge of a Police Station such as a Sub-Inspector/Circle Inspector/ Assistant Police Commissioner etc. They have been constituted under the constitution to ensure a corrupt free Central governance of our Country. Otherwise when there was the entire Police Constabulary and huge Police Establishment, CID, etc were available to prevent lawlessness and crime, why was CBI established as a separate Central investigating agency, over and above? CBI officers – from the Director down to the Investigating Officers must realise and know that their job is far above just policing and investigating a crime committed, just like a local Police Station. Their officers must have immense judicious commonsense, administrative wisdom, extreme civil sense and social commitment. They must behave in a manner reflecting the nobility of the Central Investigation Institution that they are representing. They should be a cut above the rest of the mushrooming investigating agencies we have in our country. That is the reason why the selection of the Director of CBI is done by a committee headed by the PM, along with the Chief Justice of India and the Opposition Leader of the Parliament. Does a DGP or a State Police Chief ever go through such judicious selection process? CBI Director and their officers should realise that. When frivolous cases are put for their investigation and decision, they should be seen exposing the culprits who were behind the allegations – thus should become champions of a Just Society – thus saving the innocent victims rather than witch-hunting the innocent victims by simply following a procedure based on baseless allegations. The "back room boys" – the managers of false allegations are to be hunted out and brought to justice by CBI. Then CBI should have done justice to its inception. Then the CBI will become champions of safeguarding the integrity of the institutions, corporate sectors, government officers, public sectors and other related establishments. Vigilance should be seen as a saviour of the innocent victims and not as a cog in the hands of enemies of our society. The present law requiring a government clearance as a rule, prior to anyone pouncing on to a government servant for misconduct, is to precisely avoid such innocent government employees being labelled as corrupt for doing an exceptionally good piece of work.

In an intense competitive world as of now, propelling of false allegations as a means to tarnish the image and reputation of an otherwise competent officer will be on the increase for untold personal reasons. Our society in general and Government Corporate offices, Defence, Public Sectors and bureaucracy in particular fall prey to such gullible propaganda very easily. CBI would have done a yeoman's service if they are seen as saviour to stem this rot which is eating into our institutions, save the innocent and bring out the culprits into the open. That should be to the credit of CBI. This is the best chance of CBI to come out of their present image which is anything but desirable in our country.

The second reason for releasing this narrative is to indicate to those innocent officers, who undergo such traumatic experience of the onslaught exhorted by CBI as in my case, based on false allegations, that they should never quit the boxing arena. It is easier said than done. But, if you are indeed got caught for some wrong doings – rightly or wrongly – best is to admit it then and there, without prolonging the agony and accept the decisions. That will give you peace of mind. That will save your further life. Unwantedly prolonging the fight just to prove that you are right, when you know that you are wrong, is totally unwise. You will not win.

But if you know that you have been falsely implicated, then it is your duty to yourselves, to your families, relatives, and friends and to the Institution/

Organisation you belong to, to stand up boldly and fight it out. Like Gandhiji your fight will be sharp and focused, if you are morally correct and if truth is on your side. It will cost you huge sums of money, time, effort, sleepless nights and ostracism even from your near and dear ones which will pain you the most – but never give up. Fight it to the finish, till you are able to get back your lost recognition, respect and dignity in the society that you live in. The fight may be long – like in my case – 13 long years into my retirement – till I crushed the CBI and regained my recognition and respect in the society.

All this suffering for what – I often used to wonder; to cleanse Goa Shipyard Ltd and make it perhaps the best productive Shipyard in the Country today, but was it worth at such heavy personal cost? Yes, I say with all my heart. I say yes at the top of my voice again; I say yes with all authority; that was my duty to my Nation as an officer of the Indian Navy and as a Veteran. I am grateful to Almighty that I was given this opportunity, moral and physical strength to fight to victory and an opportunity to show my mettle to the world.

Rear Admiral BR Menon (Retd)
VSM

Contents

1

Developing an Aversion to the Indian Naval Hierarchy

That a Technical Officer of the Navy cannot become the Chief of the Naval Staff was a factor that was annoying me as soon as I became conscious of it; may be in my mid career in the Navy. No one tells you this when you join the Navy. The advertisement for attracting young talents to the Navy, which appears in the newspapers, will only tell the glossy side of an otherwise wonderful career. Merit and Merit alone counts – that was the dictum – but the best Technical Officer can only become at best the Chief of Material which is six rungs below the senior most positions of the Navy, viz Chief of Naval Staff, Vice Chief of Naval Staff, Flag Officer Commanding-in-Chief of the Western Naval Command, the Eastern Naval Command, the Southern Naval Command, Fortress

Commander of Andaman and Nicobar Islands. This was a factor that annoyed me as I grew up fairly rapidly in the Navy.

Lack of any posting as a Commanding Officer for a Technical Officer in his initial career, nulled his ability to lead a crisis later in his career when required. Leadership grows with experience. As the Director of Marine Engineering (DME) in 1991-93 at NHQ, New Delhi, I personally therefore considered creating a few new postings where Technical Officers can be put in command when they are young. It was not easy. The Executive Branch Senior officers were dead against any such move. Therefore, when the Gas Turbine Repair Bay at Visakhapatnam was conceived to repair our Russian Gas Turbines in-house than sending it to erstwhile Soviet Union/Ukraine for repairs at prohibitive costs, I felt this was an ideal opportunity for creation of a Technical establishment as an Indian Naval Ship and post a Technical Officer at the helm as its Commanding Officer. To make a convincing presentation indicating the dire need of revamping the morale of the Technical Officers, was a task of a different dimension, which I had to explain to the Executive hierarchy of the Navy, the need for creation of the Repair Bay having been fully established earlier. As the Director of Marine Engineering I felt it compelling on me to prepare a paper and make a presentation on that subject alone. Vice-Admiral IC

Rao (Retd) was the Chief of Material and I made the presentation first to the Material Branch in 1992. It was included for presentation in the Commanders Conference. Conversion of the Gas Turbine Repair Bay into an Indian Naval Ship (Establishment) with a Technical Commanding Officer on its helm was the subject matter of the paper. To explain the urgent need for revamping the sagging morale of young bright Technical Officers to the peers of the Navy, was something most difficult. As DME, it was my moral authority and responsibility, however unsavoury it may be to the listeners. The presentation became an allergy to the members of the Commanders Conference. I vividly recall except Admiral L Ramdas who was the Chief of the Naval Staff who chaired the Conference, all the C-in-Cs attending the Commanders Conference refused conversion of the Repair Bay into an Indian Naval Ship. The CNS having known me well enough earlier and my view points of the dire need of developing the Technical Officers' leadership abilities in the young age itself, which I used to explain in all possible forums when I was the Commodore Superintendent of the Naval Ship Repair Yard at Kochi when Admiral Ramdas was Commander-in-Chief of Southern Naval Command, kept quiet in the Conference. The Commander-in-Chief of the Eastern Naval Command aired his view that even the total number of officers and staffs appointed to the Repair

Bay then namely 6 officers, 26 artificers and 24 MEs were not adequate to create the establishment as an Indian Naval Ship. I retorted immediately stating that only a month ago INS Rajali, was created at Arkonam as a Flying Station with 4 officers, 10 seniors and 6 juniors Sailors. None of the Commanders-in-Chief could reply to me. CNS then tried to cajole me and told the COM that I am a "tightly strung Guitar extremely sensitive to the slightest of touch." Highly disappointed I left the Commanders Conferences by humbly stating that "I am doing something which you as a senior most faculties of our Navy should have realised and initiated. I am talking about the demoralised Technical Officers of Your Navy; that happens to be mine also." Of course my statement did not go well with the C-in-Cs, except perhaps the CNS who indeed was a cut above the rest. He knew that there existed a serious problem which needs to be addressed and resolved constitutionally – not easy at all – not even resolved now.

I did not know anything about it then but later the Commanders Conference approved my proposal to create a Technical Establishment as an Indian Naval Ship in place of the Gas Turbine Repair Bay which had already been sanctioned. I was delighted. The establishment was named as INS Eksila. Today it is one of the finest Gas Turbine Repair Bays in the South-East Asian Subcontinent.

There were a plethora of many such incidences which actually confirmed to me that the Technical Officers in the Navy will remain only as a 2nd class citizen, till the day a Technical Officer becomes the Chief of Naval Staff and also Commanders-in-Chief, in their turn as per their merit and seniority. Such a possibility was unthinkable to the Navy, and even now. Seriously those days I thought of moving out of the Navy, join politics and try to become somebody in the Defence Ministry such as the Defence Minister or State Defence Minister and be in a position to dictate terms with the Naval hierarchy. The truth is, such ill-treatments to the Technical Officers are also extremely visible in the Air Force and in the Army today. Well-respected Navies of advance countries such as USA, Russia, Japan and China to an extent had changed the age-old traditions where merit and technical knowledge now matters more than the branch consciousness. We, however, still follow the old British traditions. Most of the other Commonwealth Countries also follow the British traditions of keeping the "Technical Officers under a tight leash" so to say. Sad but true.

The culmination of this was when I became the Chief Staff Officer (Technical) of the Western Naval Command at the age of 50 as a Rear Admiral (Technical). The ships of the Navy were repaired in the Naval Dockyard at Bombay under the Admiral Superintendent (ASD) who is a Vice-Admiral Technical

Officer – perhaps the senior most Technical Officer in the Navy, only next to the Chief of Material at NHQ, New Delhi. In the daily morning meetings with the Commander-in-Chief, I realized that it was a pattern to find fault with the repair and other technical procedures of the Naval Dockyard for the non-availability of ships, and squarely put the blame on the ASD, Bombay. There was a plethora of other factors like inadequate availability of spares, poor quality of spares, wrong operating practices by users, incorrect ship handling, etc etc – well apart from other HRD related issues which led to non-availability of ships. I realized that there was a tendency to sideline all these and to blame the ASD, Bombay for anything and everything. The Chief of Staff, along with his band of executive officers who attend the meetings, with the tacit support of the Commander-in-Chief, always blamed the ASD and I, as the Chief Technical Advisor of the Commander-in-Chief was supposed to support these views. On many occasions I found it difficult to support issues which are not based on merit or proof. On the contrary, non-availability of ships was due to many other factors other than inadequate or improper repair of ships. These morning meeting battles went on for a year which proved to me that I cannot continue this pattern of professional life. If I did not agree with the C-N-C's view, which is generally biased and supporting the executive officers, I was found wrong.

How I wished during those moments that the Commander-in-Chief of the Naval Command was a Technical Officer. Since the Technical Officers were a second class citizen in the Navy to a large extent, I could not serve in a system where the best cannot become the Number One and enjoy the immense benefit received by the CNS, VCNS and other Commanders in Chief of the Navy such as, while on duty they could fly in their own aircrafts, etc etc.

2

Escape from the Indian Navy

For the reasons mentioned in the above paragraphs, I waited for an opportunity to escape from the Navy without causing any damage to my career. That was not easy. Being on a fast track growth in the engineering branch and already got stamped as a competent, aspiring Technical Officer, release from the Navy was also not easy. Therefore when the post of Chairman and Managing Director of Goa Shipyard Ltd fell vacant, I applied and got selected through the Public Sector Selection Board. Managing the trouble-torn Goa Shipyard under the Defence Production Department of the Ministry of Defence efficiently, was also the foremost requirement of the Indian Navy. The Navy therefore gladly let me go. Thus I left the Navy prematurely and joined the Goa Shipyard Ltd as its Chairman and Managing Director on 7th November 1994. Here I would like to narrate an incident to make my point of the discrimination suffered by a Technical Admiral. After my selection as CMD of GSL, I still continued for nearly 2 months as the Chief Staff Officer (Technical) of the Western Naval Command. Being a Junior Rear Admiral it was the duty to see off Senior Vice-Admirals from Naval Headquarters and Commands visiting the Western Naval Command. I was thus nominated once to see off Vice-Admiral S Chand, the then VCNS, who was returning after visiting the Command. While walking with him along with his wife Mrs Pushpa Chand to his Naval Aircraft, he asked me why am I leaving the Navy. He also then said, "You are one of the finest Technical Officers I have come across Ravi and if I was the CNS, I would have not let you go." I had served under him as the Dy Director-General (Technical) of the Seabird project in Karwar for 2 years when he was the DG; so he knew me well. I replied to him "Sir, you are saying I am one of the finest Technical Officers you have known. Can I ever do in the Navy what you are now doing – flying in your own aircraft even if I become COM? No, such privileges are given to Technical Admirals. It is for such and many other discriminations, I am leaving the Navy that I love most. These discriminations have been institutionalised in the Navy, Sir. Navy cannot change it now." Admiral Chand was tongue tied. Pushpa felt sad and perhaps felt Admiral Chand should not have asked such a question. She perhaps understood then why Technical Officers with pride and self esteem cannot stick to the Navy for long. I have never met Admiral Chand again. But, I am sure he has narrated this incident to his boss, the then CNS Admiral Shekhawat. Two months later when there was a sailing regatta in Goa in early 1995 where GSL was hosting the dinner, I met the CNS as CMD of GSL. As soon as he met me, he took me aside and told me that he does not agree that Technical Officers are being discriminated in the Navy. What else can he say as CNS? I wanted to avoid any serious discussions on the matter that too between the CMD, GSL and CNS in an open forum. In any case, I did not want to embarrass the CNS because I knew if I stretched further and bring examples of discrimination against the Technical Officers in the Navy one by one, the CNS would be left tongue tied as was the case earlier with VCNS. Therefore, I changed the topic. I never met Admiral Shekhawat again.

In the Navy, I had taken part in the bombardment of Karachi as a young Engineer Officer in a Russian Missile Boat during the India-Pakistan War in December 1971. There were many other practical naval battles I fought within the Naval systems at various levels of my career but little did I realize that the major battles of my life – political and moral battles – were yet to be fought, after I left the Navy.

3

My Tryst with Goa Shipyard

Mr Shekhar Dutt, IAS was the Officiating CMD of Goa Shipyard Ltd while holding the post of Joint Secretary (Shipyards) at Ministry of Defence, New Delhi. Mr Shekhar Dutt eventually became the Defence Secretary and the Governor of the State of Chhattisgarh. He handed over the charge of GSL to me at New Delhi in his Chamber! The previous Chairman – Commodore Venkatesh (Retd) – had left the Shipyard under a cloud and vanished to America. No one in the Navy or in the Shipyard has ever heard of him, since. He ran the Shipyard well but in the end the Unions got the better of him. There were some cases against him – false or otherwise – but he was not available for any further investigation since he resigned his job and simply left the country. The Shipyard had a tremendous amount of illegitimate Union activities with the connivance of corrupt social leaders of Goa and that there were many venomous snakes in the so called garden of Goa Shipyard Ltd. These were factors never known to me nor told to me by anyone. When I took over, one thing was clear; the new Union leaders which were in power were threatened by the unauthorized Unions within and outside the Shipyard and the production output at the Shipyard were at its lowest ebb. I do not think that Mr Shekhar Dutt knew the depth of the problems in the Shipyard that he was handing over to me. He was blissfully unaware of these vital issues or had deliberately kept them away from me to prevent maligning my thought and mind, perhaps to allow me a fresh start.

After my selection as the next CMD of GSL, the then Secretary, Defence Production, Mr Vijay Kapoor, IAS, and later Lt-Governor of Delhi, on his first personal discussions with me indicated that I was handpicked by the Navy, MoD and the Public Sector Selection Board to discipline an otherwise indisciplined Shipyard for various reasons but which had tremendous prospects to grow. That was when I realized that I had a serious task ahead and I am carrying a large baggage of undefined cargo of unknown weight and dimensions. My tryst with Goa Shipyard began thus and then.

Goa Shipyard had a band of good officers, mostly ex-Navy – both Technical and Logistics – and a good set of experienced Goan workers from the shipbuilding community of Old Portuguese descent. On the face of it, they were all working sincerely. I used to make regular rounds of the Shipyard every day and looked at all the nooks and corners of the employee's conveniences, such as toilets, canteen, rest rooms, etc and gave orders for substantial improvements of these areas much before revamping the technology and techniques of modern shipbuilding and repairs. But there were many under currents beneath the silent running of the river called Goa Shipyard Ltd!

A month after my arrival, we were to launch a ship. I had inspected the launching ship the previous day, which was fitted out with all the underwater fittings such as shafts, propellers, rudders; the ship's hull was well-painted and kept ready for the launch. The lady, wife of the Chief Minister of Goa was to launch the ship and invitations were already out. The next day, on the launching day – I was informed at 7.30 AM in the morning by the General Manager (Production) of the Shipyard that one of the propellers of the ship to be launched was missing! I dashed to the side of the ship, saw it for myself, one shaft was sticking out without the propeller. It would be obvious to anyone, when the bottom of the launching ship was viewed, that one propeller was missing since the other shaft had the propeller. To prevent suspicion in the minds of the people attending the launch ceremony, I got the second propeller also removed within an hour. The propeller was of 6 ft diameter, made of bronze, cast in Goa and weighing over a tonne. At 10 AM the VIPs came and the ship was launched on time with none finding out any abnormality in both the propellers missing. We said that we will fit the propellers after the launch along with the final ship fitting out activities. In fact, this was farthest away from the truth. The propeller was stolen by a gang of people in the night. An immediate enquiry constituted by me brought to light that it was a deliberate, well-planned move by a set of people with the total involvement of the Yard employees and the security personnel at the gates of the Shipyard. The propeller could not have walked out of the Shipyard.

Private groups were always given the contract for the security of the Shipyard for decades. Unfortunately though they were under the control of the Shipyard Management, they were unionised. These security personnel were also tasked to do fire fighting in case of an eventuality. The enquiry revealed nothing. No one could be blamed or pinned down for the theft. It was a well-planned, hand in glove operation with the involvement of the Security personnel and some of the Shipyard employees, obviously for monetary benefits.

There are a string of shipyards, small and medium – along the rivers Mandovi and Zuari and they all bought materials from way side vendors – stolen or otherwise – for their ship building works. GSL being the biggest Shipyard, that too government run, was one of the sources for stealing the required materials and for reselling those stolen materials for monetary benefits at the nearby small time shipyards. This was going on for years. Couple of months later, the General Manager (Personnel) – late Cdr Akil Shaikh – had suspended a couple of employees for indiscipline. At about 11 AM in the morning, I heard uproar from the ground below CMD's office and when I looked out of the window of my office, I saw the GM (Personnel) being beaten up by a few employees and surrounded by 200 odd workers. The Security personnel were mere spectators watching the fun. I dashed down to the spot but I could not reach to help Cdr Shaikh the GM (Personnel). When I ordered the Security people, who were watching the fun to go and rescue Cdr Shaikh and apprehend the culprits, they said they cannot get involved since the Union has told them not to interfere. I then forcibly got myself into the midst, got hold of Cdr Shaikh and extricated him from the spot physically with none to help me. Thereafter, on a direct talk with the Head of the Security of the Shipyard, I realized that they are all unionized and the Unions control them, far more than the management.

4

Disciplining Goa Shipyard – Induction of CISF

These two incidents made me realize that the managers and officers of the Shipyard are simply captives of the Unions and the rebellious leaders of the Shipyard. Security was only namesake. They can do nothing in the time of a crisis as was evident. I then decided that the first thing I should do was to improve the discipline in the Shipyard and ensure safety of men and material in the Shipyard. Towards that end, the urgent need was to bring in the CISF (Central Industrial Security Force) to ensure safety and security of the Shipyard.

Within a week of this incident of the mob attack on Cdr Shaikh within the Shipyard premises, I went to New Delhi, briefed the Secretary Defence Production and the Minister concerned, went and met the Director of CISF who was a very senior IPS Officer, narrated the story to him and requested for posting of CISF personnel for the security of Goa Shipyard Ltd. The Director-General, CISF, called for the file of Goa Shipyard Ltd and after going through the old records, he indicated to me that during the past 50 years of GSL's existence, all CMDs starting from Admiral Dawson onwards had requested and tried to get CISF for GSL, but failed to do so due to extreme resistance from local Unions. In one instance, he said, the 60 odd CISF personnel who reached GSL had to be returned by the CMD at the orders of the then Labour Minister of Goa! "Do you want to try it again?", he asked me. I nodded in the affirmative. I worked out the requirement of about 78 security personnel for guarding both the gates, stores and the seaward side of the Shipyard and agreed with the terms and conditions, signed the documents and got a promise from the Director-General CISF that within 15 days he will post the CISF personnel to take over the safety and security of Goa Shipyard Ltd. This was headlines in the Goan newspapers such as *The Herald*, *The Navhind Times* and *Gomantak*. Couple of days later when I flew back to Goa, I was *gheraoed* at the airport by GSL workers spearheaded by the Unions and only with the assistance of Goa Police, I managed to reach my home – Shipyard House – which was also under *gherao* by the workers. That was the beginning of my long battles with the indisciplined GSL workers.

The 78 CISF personnel arrived in different batches as pre-arranged and they were put up at different Police camps in Goa until we found boarding place for all of them and in one fine morning, on my orders, they were placed at their positions in GSL and the existing security personnel were relieved of their posts and were given fire fighting duties only – which was part of their mandate. The entire 2,000 odd workers of GSL stuck work and they intimidated the Management through newspapers that "We are out since CISF is in. If CISF is out, we will be in."

Only officers attended the Shipyard for the next two months. It was surprising to find that not a single officer knew how to start the shop machines or operate the equipments which were under them. All these functions were done by the workers previously. There was no power. They could not even put on the switches for power. There was no water, there was no gas, there was not one machine running. None knew how to start the basic functions of the Shipyard. Slowly but surely one by one, I along with other officers, learned the locations of the switches, sequences and methods of starting machines after machines, generators after generators and within a week's time, the Shipyard started functioning in its normal way. This was the biggest blessing in disguise;

an indirect benefit that came our way enabling the managers and officers of the Shipyard to basically start and give life to the Shipyard without the help of age old, well-trained and experienced workers of the Shipyard. The ship officers gained tremendous self confidence. The strike continued for two months.

The induction of CISF brought in tremendous self-respect and confidence to the officers in GSL. For the past many years, they were subjected to humiliation and insubordination by the workers without any remedy. The CMDs and GMs were only silent spectators to the indiscipline happening inside the Shipyard till then. The various local political leaders used to meet me with the hope of persuading me to withdraw the CISF. The culmination of that was that the Chief Minister of Goa himself once called me to his office and there I was surprised to see all the Union leaders of the striking faction of the Shipyard sitting. The Chief Minister then narrated their version of the complaint. It primarily focused on the extra financial burden on the company due to the induction of CISF and the existing security staffs were deprived of their functions. I replied that the previous private security staffs were recruited for security and fire fighting duties and they were now assigned only the fire fighting duties because of the expansion of the Shipyard and the need for giving wider fire cover to many ships under construction. Instead of taking additional personnel for fire fighting duties, I had removed their extra function of security of the company. All of them can now concentrate on fire prevention and fire fighting duties. As Chairman and Managing Director of the Shipyard, it is my responsibility to ensure a fire-free and secure atmosphere in the company. No way will I permit a lax security. I told the Chief Minister that so many foreign nationals were hanging around in Goa; if there is a bomb blast or terrorist act inside the Shipyard, only I will be finally answerable to the Central Government and not the Chief Minister of Goa! I remained obdurate on my position. The strike continued and the CISF continued to man the security gates of the Shipyard.

The Member of Parliament of southern part of Goa where the Shipyard is situated – Mr Churchill Alemao came to my office soon thereafter and asked me for a huge financial help to support his election campaign which was round the corner. Naturally I declined to give any help since it was never possible to do any such thing in a Public Sector Undertaking, even if the seeker of help was the Prime Minister of India. The MP in his speech at Sada on the next day towards mobilizing his followers had publicly announced that "removal of the CMD of Goa Shipyard" as the first item of his manifesto, if elected. Locking out the Shipyard by me in view of the strike initiated by the

Unions, had made me an inveterate enemy of majority of the Vasco residents, since GSL was the source of income for most of them and because of the lock-out, they found it difficult to eke out a living. Everyone in Vasco wanted me out of the Shipyard. The MP's promise was received well by the locals, therefore, eventually, Mr Alemao won the elections and became the MP from South Goa where GSL is situated. And he tried his level best with the help of the Union leaders, to make my life miserable. I must admit he did succeed very well.

After one month of strike, the workers started to feel the pinch; the Vasco shops stopped giving them provisions, groceries, etc on credit since there was no monthly pay coming into the employees to pay up the debts to the shops at the end of the month. More and more of them started into angling and fishing in the local rivers to sustain themselves. Schools re-opened and the workers found it difficult to meet the expenses of books, tuition fees, school uniforms, etc. I was called up by the Chief Minister of Goa again along with the Home Minister and Finance Minister of the State and they ordered me to call off the lock-out and allow the workers to come into work. I narrated to them that I never stopped them from coming to work. It was they who went out of the Shipyard ever since the security gates were guarded by the CISF. They are always welcome to come back and start work. The

Ministers then told me that what I am doing is against the wishes of the employees and that the CISF should be withdrawn and *status quo* maintained. I told them point blank that I am a Public Sector servant directly responsible to the Central Government in New Delhi for its running, discipline, safety and performance. I am paying the necessary land tax, building tax, etc to the State Government. There is no cause for any grievance by the workers which alone can be raised by the State Government such as disparity in pay or salary not given to the workers on time, etc. Therefore, I said, that the State Government has no role to play except to infuse wisdom into the minds of the Union leaders and the workers and tell them that what they are doing is illogical and against the principles of justice and rule book of the Yard. No worker has been removed and the workers should voluntarily get back to work and normalcy should be established, I told the Ministers. That meeting ended in a spectrum of confrontation between the Ministers of the State and the Management of Goa Shipyard Ltd. The State Ministers may have spoken directly to the Defence Minister, since a couple of days later, I was called by the then Defence Minister, Shri Mulayam Singh Yadav to Delhi to get first-hand information on the ongoing strike which was nearing 2 months.

Mr Mulayam Singh Yadav had a nasty habit of talking only in Hindi to South Indians who did not understand Hindi. He started the conversation in high flown strong Hindi and was wholly pleased and surprised when I replied to him in equally chaste Hindi to most of his questions. This was, in view of my abundant knowledge of Hindi acquired through the initial learning of Hindi in Ajmer where I was born, and also through the day to day interactions with the Navy crowd during my time in the Navy. He told me that he was requested by the Chief Minister of Goa to call off the lock-out and send the CISF back to Delhi. I narrated the whole story again to the Defence Minister and told him that I am willing to resign and go rather than sending back the CISF. I have been handpicked by the Central Government to discipline an otherwise indisciplined Shipyard, I said, and the most vital step I have taken was to bring in the CISF. The Defence Minister knew that I was right, serious and mine was not an empty threat. He asked me how long I thought the workers will continue the strike and I told him, "I think they may go on for one more month at best and then hunger and their inability to survive will overcome their ego and illogical arguments and they will come to terms. Sir, I will not withdraw the CISF; you can withdraw me from the post of CMD. There is no war with Pakistan now that you want me to produce warships in a hurry. Allow me to tie up the loose ends at the Yard, bring in discipline that will automatically improve the production to the desired extent enabling rapid warship building process in the otherwise turbulent Shipyard. Have patience and allow me to cleanse the system." Mr Mulayam Singh stared at me for a few seconds and told me in chaste Hindi – "Okay, you may go but please make sure that you do not back out ever till the cleansing of the Shipyard in your desired manner is completed. Once the job is done, let me know." I returned to Goa.

All the Unions and the local ministers expected me to succumb to their pressure and call off the forced lock-out of the Shipyard by the workers themselves. We, officers of the Shipyard, went on doing the routine paper work, replying to all and sundry parliamentary questions while the production remained nil. Nearly a month later, ie 3 months after the lock-out and the beginning of the strike, the Labour Minister of Goa, Mr Luzine Feleiro called me and said that the Union would like to discuss their grievances with me. I told him that I do not discuss grievances of my workers with the Labour Minister of the State. If they have any grievances they can come to my office and advance their grievances. I did not go. Two days later some of the Union leaders came to my office, walking through the CISF guarded gates, under the AK-47 guns and bayonets and signing the Visitors' Book before entry. They said that they will not resist the CISF and workers may be allowed to come to work. I insisted that some Union leaders cannot sign for the workforces who are under different Unions. The strike was total for the last 3 months and therefore every worker before entry should sign in the register kept at the gate wherein there is an Undertaking written at the top of the register that from now on "I shall fully obey and will be guided by the Conduct and Discipline Rules of the Shipyard and will not destroy government property on any pretext and will advance grievances, if any, through the time honoured system available in the Shipyard, through the HR Department." The Union leaders did not agree.

The Union leaders were clever enough to devise a new strategy to appease the Goan people. Instead of the CISF, they said, there should be a GISF (Goa Industrial Security Force) which will generate employment for the local Goans. Instead of paying the CISF, they said, the Goa Government can start a GISF and the CMD of GSL can employ them as security personnel of the Shipyard. Though it looked quite ludicrous in the beginning, somehow or other, the Goan Ministers got impressed or was influenced by the Union leaders and they took up the case first with me and then with the Central Government. I of course rejected it outright since I had no authority to employ anyone else other than the Industrial Security Forces of the Central Government. The Central Government did not even reply to their letter and the strike continued.

5

Surrender of the Unions – Accepting CISF as *Fait Accompli*

A week passed. Then a few employees entered the Yard after signing the Undertaking and started working in their respective departments after marking their attendance. Slowly but steadily within the next 10 days majority of the worker had entered the Shipyard and started working. When I knew that at least 95% had returned to work and when the workers started demanding their previous 3 months' pay, I put up a Notice stating that "by not working and absenting from the Shipyard for the past 3 months on their own accord, as per many Supreme Court judgments you have not earned any pay. No Work No Pay is the order of the Apex Court. Therefore, you have not earned your pay for the last 3 months." That afternoon I was witness to a bashing of the Union leaders by the workers in the same grounds where, as I narrated earlier, I saw the bashing of the GM (Personnel) by the goons of the Union, for suspending a few indisciplined workers. However, this time the workers were bashing up the Union leaders who had misled them and the end result was loss of pay to the poor workmen for 3 months. That was the best lesson I had taught the workers of GSL and the best lesson they learned in their life. The indiscipline in the Shipyard came to a grinding halt and the induction of the CISF (which was attempted by many previous CMDs without success) had come to stay, paving way for much advanced safety and security mainly to the officers and the officers in turn were able to enforce much required discipline and techniques to improve production. And production improved rapidly.

THE NAVHIND TIMES

FRIDAY, AUGUST 30, 1996

CISF takes over security in GSL

By A Staff Reporter

PANJIM, Aug 29: The Central Industrial Security Force (CISF) was today inducted in the Goa Shipyard Ltd (GSL) in Vasco for the security of the strategically important defence public sector unit.

The GSL employees union has decided to oppose the induction by launching an agitation tomorrow.

Sources said that the induction of CISF was done quite swiftly between 2.30 to 3 p.m. when the Shipyard Employees Union leaders were about to leave for Panjim to hold a press conference against the induction of the central security force.

Justifying the induction of CISF in place of the local security force, the GSL management said "there were compelling reasons" for handing over the security from GSL's own security guards to the CISF. The four reasons listed by it in a press note issued by the PIB, include "serious security threat at GSL as perceived by the intelligence, due to the belligerent neighbours", large influx of foreigners in Goa, the prerequisities of the transfer of technology from sensitive nations an unsuitable urban location with a big open water front. The decision is purely on safety basis and in national interest, it stated.

The management claimed that over the last one year, it had tried to sensitise the union and the workers about the need for induction of the CISF.

6

Harmonising with the Workers – All Round Growth – Increase in Productivity

Nonetheless the Shipyard employees felt humiliated and were visibly angry with me and rejoiced when there were problems for the Management at the production stages or when not getting sufficient orders for Ship building. My task thereafter now was to improve the workers' acceptability of the management in general and the CMD in particular. This was not an easy task. First and foremost, by a CMD's order, I declared that I will only talk to the heads of the Unions who are employees of GSL and not to any outside Union leaders. This infuriated the local MLAs, MPs and others who were misleading the poor workers by pretending to be their saviours for their own selfish needs. But fortunately, having learned a lesson and knowing my strong resolve by now, the workers realized that there is a valid point in my argument that Union leaders must be elected from among the workers themselves and should be paid by the Shipyard Management. The Management helped in forming groups of smaller areas of work, workers were counselled, representatives were elected and from them the President, General Secretary and other Office Bearers of the Unions were elected in a free and fair manner – perhaps for the first time in the history of GSL. These elected leaders had a free access to me and could come to my office or home and advance their grievances at any time. I had created a Grievance Resolving Cell within the Shipyard under the Personnel Department and ensured that all their legitimate grievances were solved in the shortest possible time and details explained to the employees who brought it up. This system worked wonders. Within a year, my image amongst the Shipyard employees changed from one of an autocrat to that of a democrat leader but rooted in rules, ethics and justice.

Though my respect and image inside the Yard improved, outside leaders who could not any more benefit by fooling the workers, started politically plotting to dislodge me.

As the production improved the financial position of the employees also improved through bonus, etc. I ensured that employees got bonus matching to their production.

GSL — a shipyard which gives a bonus

A Public Sector company declaring a 55 per cent dividend? And topping that by giving a 1:2 bonus to its shareholders? This may appear to be a pipedream but there is in existence such a company in India. And that too a shipyard.

The pride of the Defence Ministry, Goa Shipyard Ltd (GSL) has been producing miraculous output and results for the past three years. It sales during 1996-97 soared a phenomenal 106 per cent. It not only maintained its over-50-per cent dividend of the previous year but improved on it. The sugar coating on the company's sterling performance has been the declaration of a 1:2 bonus. Goa Shipyard is perhaps the only Public Sector company to declare a bonus.

Goa Shipyard is located about 200 miles south of Bombay on the southern banks of the Zuari river in the beautiful harbour of Goa. It is one of the three public sector shipyards under the Ministry of Defence, the other two being the Mazagon Dock at Bombay and the Garden Reach Shipbuilders and Engineers on the Hooghly.

Goa Shipyard was started during the Portuguese regime as a small ship repair facility. After the 1961 liberation action the yard was left in a state of disrepair for a number of years until it was decided to revive the yard as a shipbuilding facility in 1966. The yard was placed under the control of the Ministry ofDefence. At first Goa Shipyard was a subsidiary of Bombay's Mazagon Dock but later was converted into an independent and autonomous entity.

Over the years the Indian government has invested a considerable amount in the yard to develop its facilities, to modernise the equipment and to enlarge the original scope of the yard. Today Goa Shipyard boasts of the most modern facilities and has fully repaid the trust placed in it by the government.

Over the past five years Goa Shipyard has made considerable progress in both diversification, modernisation and production. The company achieved a turnover of Rs 130.38 crore during 1993-94 which was an increase of over 244 per cent over the turnover of 1989-90. During the same period the profit increased five fold from Rs 7.14 crore to Rs 37.57 crore. The shipyard has been rated as "Excellent" in the Defence Ministry's annual assessment for the past three years.

In 1995, Goa Shipyard handed over the first of the three state-of-the-art missile boat (Type 1241 RE), INS *Vidyut*, to the Indian Navy. The remaining two were handed over in time at yearly intervals. The missile boats were the most sophisticated vessels built by the yard. The vessels are powered by gas turbines which gives them speeds in excess of 30 knots. The ships are armed with both surface-to-surface and surface-to-air missiles well as medium and close range guns. The construction of such a sophisticated vessels marked a major milestone in Goa Shipyard's progress from a small shiprepair yard to a most modern ship construction facility capable of producing up-to-date ships.

INS Prahar, the third missile vessel built by Goa Shipyard

Rear Admiral Ravi Menon

The man behind the exhilerating performanve of the shipyard is its Chairman and Managing Director, Rear Admiral Balakrishna Ravi Menon. Fifty four year old, Menon joined the Indian Navy in 1965 and had an outstanding career before retiring to head the Goa Shipyard.

Admiral Menon is a graduate of the Senior Defence Management course as well as the National Defence College, New Delhi. During the three years at the helm of affairs of the shipyard Menon has totally transformed the once staid shipyard. The shipyard, once known for its perpetual labour problems, is today humming with activity. The pride and self confidence of its emplyees has been restored.

During the present recession, when shipyards in the country are crying out for orders and work, Goa Shipyard has maintained a full order book. It has produced missile boats and survey ships for the Indian Navy, Offshore Patrol Vessels for the Coast Guard and tugs and harbour craft for the port trusts. As a sideline, it also built a Sail Training ship for the Indian Navy (See cover). It is also one of the few yards to secure orders from abroad. Last year it delivered a tug, *Veeru*, to the Maldivian Port Authority.

Yet, Menon has not been resting on his laurels. Knowing fully well the fickleness of shipbuilding business he has wisely decided to diversify. GSL has entered into a collaborative agreement with a prestigious foreign manufacturer of cranes, Rijsdijk Intergroup Services of the Netherlands. As a result of the agreement the shipyard had secured its first export order for two cranes for the private sector Gujarat Pipavav Port. The crane venture will keep GSL's order book full and maximise capacity utilisation.

Due to their age old tradition, more and more workers got addicted to alcohol. Drinking during working hours was on the increase. I then decided to introduce breath analyser test and the CISF was charged with the task of doing the tests when the workers came in the morning and when the workers returned to the Yard after lunch in the afternoon. Drinking was more during the lunch break and most of the Goan workers had a peg or two during lunch. I also had to do routine check inside the work place and those found drunk by the breath analyser were forcibly removed and appropriate pay cut was ensured. Those who were found drunk while coming to work were not permitted to enter and they lost that day's pay. All these were possible thanks to the induction of CISF. These steps reduced drinking at work and drunken workers entering and working in the Shipyard to a great extent but I realized that the output especially in the Hull Shop – welding and fabrication – had not improved. This surprised me as well as the other officers. I then put the Medical Department to look into the reason for the slackness of the workers of the Hull Shop and it was revealed after an in-depth examination, that most of the experienced and good workers can only function at the peak of their efficiency after they consume sufficient alcohol. Their hands used to shiver if they did not have a peg or two. I continued to accept the low production from the shop floor but continued enforcing breath analyser tests, as advised by the Doctors of the Shipyard, even more strictly and after six months the alcoholic workers became non-alcoholic and were producing good results. In fact, my wife – Promila Menon – in the meanwhile spearheaded a campaign to educate the workmen's wives. She created an organization with the workmen's wives and heard their grievances and 99% of the grievances were related to alcoholism and subsequent huge expenditure on liquor by their husbands, leaving little for family needs. Hence the exercise that I had undertaken not only improved the health of the workers and raised their productivity, but it also improved the happiness in their families many fold. My wife's organization established a tie-up with one Father Joe Pereira of Kripa Foundation, the Head of Alcoholics Anonymous in Bombay and he used to come down to Goa and counsel the alcohol habituated workers in the Shipyards. This action of my wife to regulate the alcoholic workers within the Yard and forcing them to drop their habits and advice their families on the perils of alcoholism brought in bonhomie and great appreciation of the workers with the management of the Shipyard. This acceptance by the workers of the management was most disliked by those who previously benefited from the Shipyard such as outside Union leaders, MLAs, MPs, etc. In the meanwhile, my act of cleansing had also moved from the Shipyard to

GSL office in Delhi. The Delhi Office was run by a Manager, one Mr Sharma. From the initial days itself, I realized that he was mismanaging the office and there was no financial discipline at all. For some reason or other, he managed to survive and be in the good books of the Director (Finance) and former CMDs of the Shipyard. There was also a Steno in Delhi Office, one Miss Vandana Jingan. She hardly knew any stenography and was just a complementary person accommodated by the Manager, Delhi Office. During my initial stages in GSL, I used to visit Delhi Office very frequently and I realized that it was mismanaged and over staffed. I therefore decided to shift the steno, Miss Vandana Jingan to the Head Office in Goa. First she represented against the transfer. Thereafter Mr Sharma represented against the transfer on one pretext or other. On my insistence, the Director (Finance) called for the entire audit of accounts of Delhi Office and that report indicated to me that all is not well at Delhi Office. There were huge advances taken by Mr Sharma which were not reconciled for years. I am still at a loss to understand how this financial mismanagement was allowed to continue at the Delhi Office by the previous administration. Under my directions, the Director (Finance) started asking for explanations and eventually it ended up in an enquiry. Miss Jingan did not obey the transfer orders but continued to defy the same and as per company's rules she was suspended and later removed from the books of the company. In connivance with Mr Sharma, she then concocted a story that I had made advances to her and since she would not respond she was removed from the company. She also made out that the transfer to Goa was aimed at putting her in the CMD's office. All these were farthest from the truth germinating from the vicious mind of Mr Sharma who was already in the docks for financial irregularity. Miss Jingan then wrote letters to the Secretary, Defence Production, and to the National Women's Commission in Delhi alleging my misbehaviour and requesting eventually for cancellation of the transfer order to Goa, saying that the transfer was only an act of harassment by me for her not agreeing to my desires. The National Women's Commission did not find any evidence and dropped the case. The Secretary Defence Production, after a preliminary enquiry by the then Joint Secretary, Shipyards, Mr Shekhar Dutt also dropped the matter as there was no evidence to prove the allegations. By then, the senior officers of the Ministry knew the game being played by Mr Sharma. The Shipyard Management then moved against her to take disciplinary action for misrepresenting facts against the CMD. Since she did not move to Goa, her salary payments were stopped. Having failed, both at the government level and the National Women's Commission, Miss Jingan with the help of Mr Sharma, the Delhi Office Manager, filed a case against me in the Magistrate Court of Delhi for sexual harassment. Once the case was accepted in the Court, I had to willy-nilly fight it. It was the saddest moment of my life to fight against an alleged sexual harassment case by one of employees of GSL, schemed and engineered by the Delhi Office Manager. In the meanwhile Miss Jingan left India and went to USA on a Work Visa but the case continued in the Court in Delhi and Mr Sharma took responsibility of conducting the case in its entirety, in her absence. And he did it for 6 years – 2 years when I was CMD and 4 years after my retirement from GSL.

As the CMD of GSL, I had no other option but to contest the case, engaging a lawyer at Delhi. Basically the case was not filed on merits, but only to harass me and the GM (Personnel) Cdr Shaikh who was also made the second accused. The pattern of the case was that the Court would send notice to both of us to appear on a specified date in the Court at Delhi. We would both travel to Delhi – I from Cochin and Shaikh from Goa – only to be told that the Complainant had not come. Some lawyer engaged by Mr Sharma would then give an affidavit saying that he is representing the Complainant and we had the responsibility to prove that the affidavit is false. The Court would go on sending summons from time to time and every time we would go to Delhi only to be informed that the Complainant was not present. Little did Cdr Shaikh and I realize that the lawyer engaged by us to fight our case had already been approached by my enemies had compromised obviously for monetary gains. It took us couple of years to find out that our lawyer was not honest and sincere in his approach to our case but was merely prolonging the case month after month just to harass us. This continued till I left GSL. On retirement, I still had to fight this case by engaging a Senior Lawyer at Delhi who eventually took the case to the High Court and proved that the Complainant had not appeared even once during the 3 years after filing the case. True to the culture of Public Sector, since the case began as a retort to the CMD's cleansing efforts, the legal expenses for this case even after my retirement were paid by GSL, fortunately. Mr Sharma had been pursuing the case with vengeance, having been first suspended and then removed by me from the company for financial misappropriation. I was indeed surprised to realize that before my arrival, Mr Sharma was heading the Delhi Office for over a decade indulging in large scale financial improprieties without being caught. He could not swallow the fact that I moved strictly as per law and the Rule Book of GSL, proved his guilt and removed him from the company. Even after his removal from GSL, I understand he is even now engaged in fighting the case legally against GSL for his financial misappropriations and he had not returned the dues to the company, still – as I understand.

At GSL my efforts continued in establishing discipline and bringing up the productivity of the company. Our productivity grew and GSL became one of the first Public Sector Shipyards in India to give Dividend Warrants to the government. It was with greatest of pride that I gave a cheque to Mr Mulayam Singh Yadav the then Defence Minister and who received it with great pleasure. Handsome bonuses were given to the workers for their sincere efforts in bringing up the productivity of the company. With unflinching efforts at every level, GSL received large amount of ship building orders from within the country and one export order for a Tug to the Republic of Male in 1997. That was perhaps the first export order received by an Indian Public Sector Shipyard from a foreign country. In the Shipyard, discipline was in place, addiction of workers to liquor was brought down and GSL became a happy family.

Housing being the biggest issue for the workers, I managed to get large tracts of government land from the Chief Minister, Mr Pratap Singh Rane for starting a housing colony for GSL workers. Even sanctions for electricity and water connections were received. During the Goa Governor's address on Republic Day, the exemplary manner in which GSL was being run, found

Economic Times.

ET 23.2.95

Govt-run Goa Shipyard casts anchor in global waters

Prakash Kamat

PANAJI 21 FEBRUARY

GOVERNMENT-RUN Goa Shipyard Ltd (GSL), heading the Indian shipbuilding consortium bidding for the Royal Malaysian Navy Patrol Vessels programme, is hopeful of the consortium getting shortlisted.

According to chairman and managing director of GSL, Rear Admiral (Retd) Balakrishnan Ravi Menon, who led the delegation of the Indian consortium as the head of the lead yard to Malaysia recently, in all 34 shopyards have submitted tenders.

The tender, worth billions of dollars, will be shortlisted within two months. Should the Indian consortium manage to get it, it would be one of the major Indo-Malaysian combine defence projects, Mr Menon said.

The project involves building a large number of patrol vessels for the Royal Malaysian Navy in their Dockyard at Lumus, Malaysia. While Mazgaon Dock Ltd and GRSE would form the ship design and ship building part of the consortium, Bharat Electronics Ltd (BEL), Bangalore, will assist GSL with high-tech electricals and electronics support.

Development Consultants Ltd and Tata Consultancy Services are part of the consortium in helping GSL develop infrastructure in the Malaysian dockyard for building high-tech offshore patrol vessels.

Tata Consultancy Services would give necessary assistance through GSL for integrated logistic support systems and other software engineering application to Malaysia.

Meanwhile, GSL will also be among the Indian participants at the five-day International Defence Exhibition (INDEX '95) show in Abu Dhabi (UAE) beginning from March 19, Mr Menon said.

He said major arms manufacturers of the world, including India, would vie to get a share of the $ five billion Gulf military market when they display their latest weaponary at the show.

a mention which was a rarity. In recognition of my efforts, the Chief Minister of Goa recommended me for a Padma Shri to be awarded by the President of India. But I had no political pull in the Prime Minister's Office. In India merit alone does not matter! Thus the Goa Chief Minister's recommendation for awarding me a Padma Shri was turned down at the highest level. I am not privy to the reasons for the rejection.

CITATION

Rear Admiral B.R. Menon retired from the Navy in Nov 94 after a distinguished career of over 30 years. He took over the Chairmanship of Goa Shipyard at a time when work had come almost to a standstill, the management was in disarray and discipline amongst the work force was at its lowest ebb.

2. By sheer determination, tenacity of purpose and dint of hard work, Admiral Menon set about the task of placing Goa Shipyard in the frontline of warship production in the country. Towards this end, he thoroughly streamlined the administration, modernised the work force, improved the work ethics and brought in high productivity and scientific methodologies - first time in the country - such as "modular construction" of ships through Technology Transfer from the leading shipyards in Portugal. As a result, Goa Shipyard has become the first Public sector Shipyard in India to have won an 'export order' in the last 15 years for a ship - indeed a commendable achievement since the export order was achieved without any Government subsidy whatsoever by Goa Shipyard. The productivity of the shipyard has been unprecedented during his tenure as the Chairman & Managing Director resulting in Goa Shipyard having been upgraded by the Govt to Schedule 'B' from Schedule 'C'. This has enhanced the prestige and prosperity of Goa itself since Goa Shipyard is the largest Industry employing the largest number of people in Goa.

3. The excellent order book position that Admiral Menon has achieved in a short span of 22 months has put the shipyard in a considerable advantage over other shipyards in India, improving its financial position. Consequently, this has improved the financial position of the satellite and auxillary Industries in Vasco in particular and in Goa in general thus helping the State unmeasurably.

4. The first tenet of warship building is instilling discipline in the workforce. In order to bring in security and discipline, Admiral Menon has been singularly instrumental in deploying the Central Industrial Security Force in Goa Shipyard - a National requirement - to improve the security and safety of this Defence public sector unit, which could not be achieved for the past decades - a task which many of his predecessors had tried and failed. The courage, moral integrity, strength of mind and the leadership qualities shown by Rear Admiral B.R. Menon in achieving the deployment of Central Industrial Security Force in Goa

Shipyard is a singular instance for recognition for him of the highest order. By this action, he not only has disciplined GSL but also has become a torch bearer to the other Industries in Goa - has set an example for others to follow.

5. Rear Admiral B.R. Menon has been an excellent Chairman, if public sectors are considered as an 'instrument of the Government policy'. [With this in view, he has been considered as the 'Man of the Masses' in Vasco.] The housing colony for the workers which was lying as in 'closed files' due to environmental non-clearance for the past 5 years, has been resurrected by him through his continuous pursuation and missionary zeal at the highest levels in the Central and State Government - thus bringing to fore the importance of 'social obligation' of a public sector for the upliftment of his work force. That, he has been able to get Central sanction for the housing colony and has contracted the same at a cost of Rs.25 crores without any outside financial help, is the highest tribute to his compassionate feelings for bringing up the lot of his employees in a Statemanly manner. Housing is a dire need of Goa State. By providing shipyard quarters to its employees, he has indeed contributed immensely to the growth and prosperity of Goa State.

6. When Public Sector Industries in India are finding it difficult to cope with the production climate in the country, in the month of March 97 alone Goa Shipyard Ltd delivered 3 large ships - one warship for the Navy, one advanced patrol vessel for the Coast Guard and the first export ship order from India - and launched one advanced offshore patrol vessel for Coast Guard. This is an unprecedented feat by any Industry in India, worthy of the highest recognition to the Chief Executive of the Company. This was only possible due to the dynamic leadership and motivational techniques of Admiral Menon and his vision. By this unparalleled productivity, Goa as a State benefitted financially substantially, elevating the lots of the people of the State of Goa. The Company also declared the highest ever dividend of 52.5% directly benefitting the shareholders - many citizens of Goa.

7. In view of his outstanding technical knowledge, Statemanly vision, missionary zeal and ability to convert visions into missions, he has been selected and put as a "visitor" of the Goa University. He has helped the University and State through technology missions at various levels.

....3

- 3 -

8. Rear Admiral B.R. Menon (Retd) has thus made Goa Shipyard a matter of pride for the people of Goa and has succeeded in bringing considerable prosperity to the citizens of the Goa and improving their lot. His corporate management of Goa Shipyard has become a lesson in corporate management in the State of Goa. In recognition of his outstanding contribution to the growth of the shipyard and to the growth of State of Goa, he is strongly recommended for the award of PADMA SHREE.

Panaji, Goa

07 April 1997

Pratapsing R. Rane
Chief Minister of Goa

OFFICE OF CHIEF MINISTER
GOVERNMENT OF GOA

7

Beginning of the Political Vendetta

All these unprecedented progress made by the Shipyard only annoyed the outside leaders including MLAs and MPs since they found in me a man who could not be pushed around. They therefore started scheming various options to oust me. In their efforts they found an ally in one Major Thomas (Retd) who was Manager (HR) of GSL but removed by the previous CMD Mr Shekhar Dutt, IAS, after being caught receiving bribes in his office from a labour contractor. Major Thomas had been fighting the case in a Goa Court while he was under suspension, when I took over. He pleaded with me for withdrawal of the case and his reinstatement in his previous post. Realising that I was not acceding to his various requests and pressure tactics, he became one of my enemies whose sole aim was my removal from the post of CMD of GSL. The GSL case against Thomas moved on as per the rules and he was removed from GSL by me 2 years after my taking over of GSL. Meanwhile those outside Union leaders headed by one Vincent Dias, ex-President of the Union were sowing the seeds of poison in the minds of the workers against me. Many a times, Vincent Dias wanted entry into the Shipyard during working hours to meet other Union activists inside, but the CISF personnel did not allow any such thing. My strict instructions were that all Union activities and Union meetings must be after the working hours; only legitimate Unions can hold meetings within the Yard after working hours; that too only with prior permission of the HR Department. Unauthorised and illegitimate Unions can have meetings anywhere else, once the workers leave the Shipyard after working hours. There were commotions galore at the CISF gate when Vincent Dias and his unholy cohorts were trying to get in but thanks to the induction of CISF, none of their attempts succeeded. This infuriated them further.

In the above scenario, as usual, my enemies gathered around with the sole aim of removal of the CMD from his post. Vincent Dias and previous Union leaders joined hands with the suspended and eventually removed Major Thomas (Retd), ex-Manager (HR) at GSL and Mr Sharma, dismissed Manager of Delhi Office. They were supported wholeheartedly in their scheming and planning by the local politicians and outside Union leaders. That was the period when Mr George Fernandes became the Defence Minister. Mr George Fernandes as is well-known, was a Trade Union Leader. He had close allegiance with Mr Churchill Alemao, the MP from South Goa. A second MP from Goa, John Fernandez was also roped into join hands in their efforts in the "Remove Menon Campaign". Letters after letters were written by the outside Union leaders to the Defence Minister Mr George Fernandes alleging many financial improprieties and indisciplinary actions committed by me. I used to get letters from Joint Secretary (Shipyards) asking explanation for each and every letter from the Unions address to Defence Minister, CBI, etc. I must admit a large part of my official time went in defending my stand and explaining my position. Looking back at it I feel during the last 2 years in GSL, almost 50% of my official time which could otherwise have been well spent for the innovative improvements of the Shipyard, was not utilized properly. Yet I paved the way for a better attendance system directly linked to the salary of the workers which helped improve the attendance of the workers to a large extent, total computerization of the Yard including production floor, e-governance, modern computerised design of ships, re-equipping the Yard with modern equipments related to production multipliers, introducing the workforce to modern ship building techniques and improving their health through better medical care and attention. All these had made the standing of GSL into a higher category and in recognition of that substantial growth, GSL was upgraded from Schedule 'C' to Schedule 'B' Public Sector Company. This upgradation helped the officers to be slotted into a higher pay scale. As the Chairman of the company, I however, remained in the pay scale of a Schedule 'C' company despite my demanding the enhanced scale, for reasons which will be explained later on in this narration. The Defence Ministry headed by Shri George Fernandes refused to upgrade me.

The Ministry of Defence was in a dilemma. The performance of the Shipyard had tremendously increased but the complaints against the CMD through various agencies and disgruntled elements with the help of local MPs especially Mr Churchill Alemao and MLAs increased many fold. The Joint Secretary (Shipyard) made several visits for on-the-spot study, as directed by the Defence Minister Mr George Fernandes and reported the good health of the Company. Various allegations of misuse of funds by me for entertaining Goan Ministers and other dignitaries in my house, procurement of improper timber for building of the first ever Sail Training Ship made for the Indian Navy – INS Tarangini – the marginal loss suffered by the Company by making this three mast wooden Training Ship for the first time in India, marginal loss made by the Company in manufacturing dockside crane as an export item to Holland, partiality shown by the CMD to various officers and workers in the Yard, were some of the major false allegations. Supporting these, as engineered by Mr Sharma from Delhi, misbehaviour with the lady clerk of Delhi also appeared. These letters originated from Goa – well-crafted by ousted Union leaders, politicians and further fine tuned by Mr Sharma in Delhi to increase the punch of misappropriation, etc and were mostly sent or hand delivered from Delhi itself to the Defence Minister and the Secretary, Defence Production. And since Mr George Fernandes owing to Union pressure from Goa used to ask about these cases with the Secretary, Defence Production, the Secretary had to examine all letters on merits and put back to him. In none of the explanations by the Secretary, I was implicated or indicted. In fact, they explained in clear terms that it is the result of Menon's disciplining the Shipyard beyond belief and improving its productivity "that was the basic reason for CMD's alleged misconduct and misdeeds emanated from the disgruntled elements of the Shipyard in particular in Vasco and Goa in general." Having not succeeded inside the Yard, there were black flag agitations outside the Yard to prevent the workers and officers from entry. I had firmly dealt with such things with the help of the Goa Police. The Intelligence Bureau had warned the Ministry of Defence that there is danger to my life. I was therefore given special protection by them in my house and in my car during my travel by CISF. This was an unprecedented instance which has never happened to any other Public Sector chief before. I only knew my programme of the day. My daily programme was never printed and kept. As usual I was advised to go for my games, which is Tennis or Squash at the nearby Naval courts unannounced and I only knew my programme, as per directions of the IB.

None of these ever bothered me or deterred me from going ahead with the task ahead and I went full steam ahead with whatever innovative ideas I had to improve the Shipyard and the lot of my workers.

8

My Tryst with CBI

Having not found favour with the Ministry of Defence, my enemies started writing to the CBI Local Office in Goa and to the CBI Director himself, alleging misappropriation of funds, siphoning off money and whatever else they could concoct. Copies of all these went to the Defence Minister, Mr George Fernandes whom they claimed as their friend. My Heads of Department and I had a tremendous task of replying, line by line, defending our position and revealing the truth. This however was not easy and always had a one sided effect. I and my officers spent large amount of working time replying to these letters and I considered this as a national waste but I had no other choice. It is human nature that when a wrong thing is stated ten times by ten different people in a similar tone and tenor, the recipient starts believing the allegations and giving credence to the views expressed. This is how the factions from Goa and Delhi eventually made the Defence Minister believe that there could be truth in the allegations but there was nothing substantial in them after an in depth probe by the Defence Ministry and hence not even a Departmental probe could be instituted against the alleged corrupt practices. In fact, my honest and extremely strong stand had indeed frustrated my enemies, perhaps including the Defence Minister, primarily a Union leader who was not able to satisfy the demands of his friendly Unions from Goa, to remove me from the post of CMD, Goa Shipyard.

There was an instance here where my action must have infuriated the CBI factions in Goa. The local CBI Head had requested my Vigilance Officer, Mr Venugopal, to give a hired car to DIG of Police, CBI Shri KP Raghuvanshi, who was visiting Goa on an official visit. With my permission, Mr Venugopal provided a car. I had strictly instructed that the driver should note where all they travel within Goa, before the papers were put up for my sanction. Three days later when the papers were put up with the driver's worksheet, it was evident that the Joint Director with his family, who arrived in Goa, had only visited the various tourist spots and beaches of Goa and not any official places at all. I am giving here a copy of CBI's letter of May 1998 asking for the vehicle for official duty. I am also attaching the worksheet details of his trip which clearly indicate the visit conducted by the car to various beaches and pleasure spots in Goa totalling a hired bill of ₹3,470. Just as a matter of interest I am also attaching here details of tour of one Mr JK Dutt, Joint Director CBI, in GOA in June 1997 when GSL provided an official car for official duties. He also had visited all entertainment centres and beaches in Goa. This is to indicate that so called CBI senior officers were in the habit of misusing the official transports allocated to them by the Public sectors with impunity. I am giving here under one or two examples of CBI's request to CMD, GSL and proof of misuse of the transport allocated by GSL.

Therefore I decided to put an end to it. Much against his wish, I made my Vigilance Officer, Mr Venugopal, who gave the car to the CBI local office in Goa, write to the local CBI Head indicating that the car has been misused by the CBI. This may have been the first instance in the history of CBI, when they were told by a Public Sector Vigilance Officer that they were wrong. They were also informed that if they did not pay the bill, the CMD will write directly to the CBI Director with proof. Within a week, the Head of CBI from Bombay called me up, apologized and said they will pay and I need not have to do anything more in the matter. The payment was effected by the CBI immediately, but the CBI both from Bombay and

SO(Adm)
Vehicle to report to CBI
office Panaji at 0830 hrs on 25/5/98

No.C/32/G-II/CBI/ACB/GOA

CENTRAL BUREAU OF INVESTIGATION
[illegible] CORRUPTION BRANCH
GOVT. OF INDIA
[illegible] Building, 1st Floor
Near Doordarshan Kendra
ALTINHO, PANAJI - GOA 403001

Dated:- 21.05.98.

To,

The Chairman Cum Managing Director,
Goa Shipyard Limited,
Vasco-Goa.

Sub. :- Request to provide vehicle.

Sir,

Shri. K.P. Raghuvanshi, Deputy Inspector General of Police, CBI, ACB, Mumbai, is visiting Goa on 25-5-98 for official purpose. As such, it is requested that an AC Car may be provided for his official movement in Goa for 3 days from 25-5-98 to 27-5-98 .

Yours faithfully,

Supdt. of Police,
CBI/ACB/GOA.

22/5

GOA SHIPYARD LTD.

Name of Driver / Owner D. Shirodkar

Date 25-5-98		**Vehicle No.** GA 02 U 2027	
TIME		**KMS**	
Opening	730 AM	**Opening**	85803
Closing	2130	**Closing**	86079

Details of the Route : VASCO To Panaji Altinho C.B.I Khorlim Railway station, old GOA, Ponda Mardol, dona Paula VASCO M.P.T. Circuit House Anjuna Vagator Beach back Panaji city M.P.T. Harbour VASCO.

Signature of Controlling Officer

GOA SHIPYARD LTD.

Name of Driver / Owner D. Shirodkar

Date 26-5-98		Vehicle No. GA 02 V 2021	
TIME		KMS	
Opening	6.00 A.M.	Opening	86080
Closing	21-00	Closing	86325

Details of the Route : VASCO To, sada, M.P.T; VASCO, Baymalo, VASCO, sada, M.P.T. VASCO, Panaji, City, Altino, Panaji, Altino, Panaji Ponda Colva Margao Panaji C.B.I Altino Panaji City. Altino To old Goa. Karmalim R. staion To back. VASCO

Signature of Controlling Officer

GOA SHIPYARD LTD.

Name of Driver / Owner D. Shirodkar

Date 27.5.99		Vehicle No. GA 02 U 2021	
TIME		**KMS**	
Opening	8.15 AM	Opening	86338
Closing	20.40	Closing	86460

Details of the Route : VASCO TO Panaji C.S.I. Altinho Panaji Mapusa M.P.T. back VASCO

Signature of Controlling Officer

HIRED CAR BILL OF GA02 V2027 28/5/98

Mr. D. Shirodkar

S.No	Date/Time	Opening/Closing kms	Total kms	Rs. Ps
1.	25/5/98 0730hrs to 2130hrs	85803 – 86079	276 km	1380-00 90.00
2.	26/5/98 0600hrs to 2100hrs	86080 – 86325	245 km	1225-00 105.00
3.	27/5/98 0830 – 2030hrs	86338 – 86460	122 km	610-00 60.00
				3470.00

(Rupees three thousand Seventy only)

The car was hired for Dy. Inspector General of Police CBI Shri C.P. Raghunathan original approval along with Logbook attached. Bill certified for payment

OIC TPR

(D. Shirodkar)

Mr. J.K. Dutt.
Jt Director/CBI/Delhi.

GOA SHIPYARD LTD.

Name of Driver / Owner Suresh Mangrekar

Date 13.06.97		Vehicle No. GA02 V 2621	
TIME		**KMS**	
Opening	35.00	Opening	49370
Closing	22.00	Closing	49668

298

Details of the Route : Vasco to panjim to althino to Sawantwaddi to rly Station to sawantwaddi to sawantwaddi rly station to mapusa to Bagu side to Calangute Beach to panjim althino CBI off to circuit guest house to panjim bus stop to vasco to panjim bus stop & back to vasco.

Signature of Controlling Officer

Used By CBI officials

GOA SHIPYARD LTD.

Name of Driver / Owner: Suresh Manjrekar

Date: 15.06.97	Vehicle No. GA 02 V 2621
TIME	**KMS**
Opening: 07.00	Opening: 49670
Closing: 22.00	Closing: 49963 (293)

Details of the Route: Vasco to panjim althino cirquit house to Bagha beach to calangute to Anjuna beach to old goa church to panjim city to Vasco mpt port to sada to vasco to panjim Mandovi Hotel to Dona paula to panjim city to fort Aguada to Bagha Beach to panjim Althino to cirquit house to C.B.I off to Cirquit House & back to vasco

Signature of Controlling Officer:

Used by CBI official

CVO

GOA SHIPYARD LTD.

Name of Driver / Owner Suresh Mangrekes

Date 16.06.97	Vehicle No. GA02 V 2121
TIME	**KMS**
Opening 07.00.	Opening 49965
Closing 22.00	Closing 50297

332

Details of the Route : Vasco to panjim to cirquit guest house to CBI off to cirquit guest house to Baga monteiro hotel to panjim to Mangueshi temple to Shantadurga temple to phodha to Margao city to Londa Rly. Station & back to panjim to vasco.

Signature of Controlling Officer

Used by CBI Officials

Goa were looking for the slightest opportunity to pounce on me and that opportunity came soon thereafter, thanks to the involvement of the Defence Minister, Mr George Fernandes.

The Defence Minister was already prejudiced against me since his mind was poisoned by various letters being written by groups from Goa and Delhi whose only aim was to remove me from the post of CMD. Mr Churchill Alemao, the MP from South Goa and Mr John Fernandez, MP from North Goa had written letters in support of various allegations against me raised by the different factions from Goa. In total Goa had only 2 MPs and both were against me for no rhyme or reason.

Some other senior politicians such as Mr Ramakant D Khalap and Dr Wilfred D'Souza supported me and wrote letters in my favour to the Defence Minister. Towards the end, the letters to the Defence Minister were also copied to the CBI Director in New Delhi.

The brains behind all these letters were the expelled Manager (Personnel) of Goa Shipyard and the expelled Manager of Delhi Office. In fact, some of the letters in Delhi were taken by the former Manager of Delhi Office who personally went to the MP's residence, got his signature and handed over the letters to the Defence Minister's office and CBI Director's office in New Delhi. I got this information through

EXH '372'

Churchill Alemao
(Ex-Chief Minister Goa)
Member of Parliament
(Lok Sabha)

... MATHURA ROAD, NEW DELHI-110 [illegible]
TEL.: [illegible] FAX: [illegible]

NOVANGULLY, VARCA SALCETTE, GOA
TEL.: [illegible]
FAX: [illegible]

Dated: 18th APRIL, 1998

Dear Shri George Fernandes ji,

I heartily felicitate you once more on your taking over as the Defence Minister of India. I admire your hard working with honesty keeping your ideals and principles. And you have been rewarded. You have ... vocal and fearless in advocating the cause of the labour force and workers and their Unions throughout the Country. I wish you every wishes both in this high Office and personal prosperity and good health, for years to come.

Enclosed please find a representation from the Shipyard Employees Union; Ref. No. SEU/DM/01 dated 16th Apr 98, which is self explanatory. I am fully aware of the difficulties faced by the workers of GSL. There is no improvement either in the functioning of this Public Sector Undertaking of the Union Govt. under the Ministry of Defence nor is there any sign of cordial relations between the Management and the Employees Union.

I feel that thorough investigation is required to set the matters right in the interests of all concerned. An enquiry by a Senior Officer of your Ministry into the conduct and style of functioning of the Chairman & Managing Director vis a vis the Union and its members is called for. Also the Goa Shipyard Ltd., needs revitalisation and change in the higher management cadres for its smooth sailing.

I shall be highly obliged if you give a thought to the above suggestions in the light of grievances expressed in the enclosed letter from the Union President and order immediate and appropriate action. The truth will come out and everyone will be happy.

With regards and best wishes,

Yours Sincerely,

(Churchill Alemao)

Shri George Fernandes,
Hon'ble Minister for Defence,
Govt. of Inida,
South Block,
New Delhi - 11 00 01

P.S. A new competent CMD will eliminate all the grievances and troubles.

MEMBER
• PARLIAMENTARY STANDING COMMITTEE ON COMMU...
• CONSULTATIVE COMMITTEE ON TOURISM

NOTE: Typescript of previous page image.

Asoka Pillar Emblem

Churchill Alemao
(Ex-Chief Minister, Goa)
Member of Parliament
(Lok Sabha)

Mathura Road, New Delhi - 110 001
Tel: 3389433 Fax: 011-3389433
Navangully, Varca, Salicette, Goa
Tel: 745281, 745139, 745126
Fax: 0834-731760, 745281

Dated: 18th April, 1998

Dear Shri George Fernandes Ji,

I heartily felicitate you once more on your taking over as the Defence Minister of India. I admire your hard working with honesty keeping your ideals and principles. And you have been rewarded. You have been vocal and fearless in advocating the cause of the labour force and workers and their Unions throughout the Country. I wish you every success both in this high office and personal prosperity and good health for years to come.

Enclosed please find a representation from the Shipyard Employees Union; Ref.No.SEU/DM/01 date Apr 98, which is self explanatory. I am fully aware of the difficulties faced by the workers of GSL. There is no improvement either in the functioning of this Public Sector Undertaking of Union Govt, Under the Ministry of Defence nor is there any sign of cordial relations between the Management and Employees Union.

I feel that thorough investigation is required to set the matters right in the interests of all concerned and style of functioning of the Chairman & Managing Director vis a vis the Union and its members is called for. Also the Goa Shipyard Ltd needs revitalisation and change in the higher management cadres for its smooth sailing.

I shall be highly obliged if you give a thought to the above suggestions in the light of grievances advanced in the enclosed letter from the Union President and order immediate and appropriate action. The truth will come out and everyone will be happy.

With regards and best wishes,

Yours Sincerely,
(Signature)
Churchill Alemao

Shri George Fernandes,
Hon'ble Minister for Defence,
Govt. of India,
South Block,
New Delhi - 110 001

PS: A new competent C&MD will eliminate all the grievances and troubles.

Fax : 250458 Jan 29 '98 01:15

EXH '373'

RAMAKANT D. KHALAP
रमाकांत दत्ताराम खलप

No.RDK/Per/98/728 Date:7th August, 1998.

Dear Shri George ji

Our friend Mr. Churchill Alemao is resorting to tactics of black mail and intimidation to coerce Admiral Menon, Chairman & Managing Director of Goa Shipyard. Recently, Mr. Alemao has publicly threatened that he will have Admiral Menon removed from his post through you, his close friends. I am sure Mr. Churchill will approach you with his demands. Admiral Menon in my opinion is a dedicated officer and has done a lot to further the interest of the Shipyard as well as his workmen. Mr. Alemao is publicly dragging your name to strengthen his clout among the workmen, some of whom he has recently used for a morcha to the Governor's palace to protest against the dismissal of Pratapsing Rane, the ex. Chief Minister.

I am bringing this to your notice to caution you against any attempts by Mr. Churchill Alemao to influence you to take action against Admiral Menon which may prove detrimental to the interests of the Shipyard and its employees.

With Warm Regards,

Yours Sincerely,

(RAMAKANT D. KHALAP)

Shri GeorgeFernandes,
Union Minister for Defence,
Govt. of India,
NEW-DELHI.

Fax - 011- 3015403
N.O.O.
Admiral Menon — 513943

Res.: 168, Altinho, Mapusa, Goa 403 507 Phone: 262708 Fax: 0832 - 250458 E-mail: khalap@bom3.vsnl.net.in
Former UNION MINISTER FOR LAW & JUSTICE
Former DY CHIEF MINISTER OF GOA
Chairman BANK OF GOA (The Mapusa Urban Co-op. Bank of Goa Ltd.)

NOTE: Typescript of previous page image.

Ramakant D Khalap
रमाकांत दत्ताराम खलप

No. RDK/Per/98/728 Date: 7th August, 1998

Dear Shri George ji,

Our friend Mr. Churchill Alemao is resorting to tactics of black mail and intimidation to coerce Admiral Menon, Chairman & Managing Director of Goa Shipyard. Recently, Mr. Alemao has publicly threatened that he will have Admiral Menon removed from his post through you, his close friend. I am sure. Mr. Churchill will approach you with his demands. Admiral Menon in my opinion is a dedicated officer and has done a lot to further the interest of the Shipyard as well as his workmen. Mr. Alemao is publicly dragging your name to strengthen his clout among the workmen, some of whom he has recently used for a march to the Governor's Palace to protest against the dismissal of Pratapsing Rane, the ex-Chief Minister.

I am bringing this to your notice to caution you against any attempts by Mr. Churchill Alemao to influence you to take action against Admiral Menon which may prove detrimental to the Shipyard and its employees.

With warm regards

Yours sincerely
(signature)
(Ramakant D. Khalap)

To
Shri Geoge Fernandes
Union Minister for Defence
Govt. of India
New Delhi
Fax-011-3015403

some friendly Union leaders of GSL who were informed of various such developments through their friends in New Delhi. The Shipyard was growing in strength and productivity because of my firm handling of the various administrative and production matters of the Shipyard, but my reputation was rapidly declining in the Goa circles and in the Ministry of Defence due to the avalanche of letters accusing me of various financial and other crimes. All these letters ended up in various internal investigations by the Ministry of Defence but nothing could be substantiated at any point and a stage had reached where even the Joint Secretaries, Additional Secretaries and Secretary of the Defence Production Department got fed up with the unsubstantiated letters and started to ignore them. I am giving here with copies of letters dated 25th August and 31st August 1998 from Shri Om Prakash, Joint Secretary (Shipyards) asking my comments on Goa Shipyard Union letters to the Defence Minister.

भारत सरकार
रक्षा मंत्रालय
रक्षा उत्पादन एवं पूर्ति विभाग
नई दिल्ली
GOVERNMENT OF INDIA
MINISTRY OF DEFENCE
DEPT. OF DEFENCE PRODUCTION & SUPPLIES
NEW DELHI

OM PRAKASH
Joint Secretary(Shipyards)

Tele: 3011219

D.O. 2297/JS(SY)/98

31st August, 1998

Dear Admiral,

A copy of the letter dated 25.8.98 addressed by Shri Vincent Dias, President Shipyard Employees Union, Goa to Hon'ble Raksha Mantri is enclosed. R.M. has desired that he may be apprised of the factual position immediately. It is requested that your comments on the enclosed letter alongwith the factual position may be furnished immedliately.

With regards,

Yours sincerely,

(OM PRAKASH)

RAdm B.R.Menon
CMD
Goa Shipyard Ltd
Goa.

Encl: As above.

00918345110?0 VASCO-DA-GAMA PAGE 01

SHIPYARD EMPLOYEES' UNION, GOA

REG. NO. 143 Phone No. : 511560

At, GOA SHIPYARD LTD., VADDEM, VASCO-DA-GAMA, GOA.

By fax no. 3015403 & By Speed Post.

Affecting

President

Monino Kulibeiro
Vice President

Teotonio D'Costa
Vice President

Suresh Parab
Vice President

Loginho Xavier
General Secretary

Jerry Jorge Damasceno
Secretary

Satish Sivenkar
Secretary

Mahesh Naik
Treasurer

Date:25th/08/98.

To
Honourable Union Defence Minister
Govt. of India
South Block, DHQ P.O.
New Delhi - 110011.

Sir,

We are deeply pained to inform you that all the workers of Goa Shipyard Ltd., a Defence Public Sector undertaking had to resort to tools down strike from 19th August 98' and the statement still continues without any signs of solution on account of the adamant and anti-labour attitude of the Company management.

Infact, we have been regularly making representations to your goodself here earlier against the bad actions of the Chairman & Managing Director RAdm. B.R. Menon. It hurts us most because the corrupt and inefficient Chief of this Shipyard still continues his acts in the same manner as in the past thereby destroying the progress of the Company.

Series of illegal suspensions of workmen since August last year which are in contravention to the Company's Certified Standing Orders, non-payment of Bonus/ Productivity Incentives for the year 1997 - 1998 claiming that the workers have not earned the same, rampant anti-labour activities/practices including refusing to entertain the elected representatives of the Union and mis-use of the Central Industrial Security Force against the workmen are some of the issues the workers are irked resulting in the present [illegible] The management has closed down the Canteen Services since 21st August for obvious reasons and against the Factory Act, 1948.

..2/-

9

Cause of CBI Raid

Giving proper replies to these letters took large part of my time and effort and that of my officers sheer waste of time and energy. In fact, in one of the file notings which I saw with the help of a Keralite staff of the Defence Minister, Mr George Fernandes had expressed his unhappiness in writing when in reply to one of the enquiries conducted based on allegations from Goa received from MPs, Secretary (Defence Production), Mr Vijay Raghavan had clearly stated that he cannot indict me at all since there is no truth in the allegations. The Trade Union moulded Defence Minister, Mr George Fernandes, wanted to hook me one way or the other to appease the Unions. Soon thereafter, I had a phone call from his office by one of the Joint Secretaries, saying that the Defence Minister is sending someone from Ranchi and that I may induct him into GSL in the IT Department. Within a day, the person arrived with bag and baggage, met me and told me he has come as per the directions of his 'Mama' Mr George Fernandes. I put a team of officers to examine his knowledge on IT area and they told me at the end of the day that let alone his knowledge on computers, he cannot even spell the word 'computer', properly. The next day, I politely turned him away saying that we will call him when there is a vacancy. He went back to Delhi and reported the matter. Indeed when I had told him to go back, he said that he is the son of the Treasurer of Mr George Fernandes's Samta Party Headquartered in Ranchi. He must have reported the matter to his 'Mama'. This was on a Thursday morning. That Friday afternoon I had a phone call from the same Joint Secretary from the Defence Minister's office intimating me that the Defence Minister is extremely disappointed at my action in not employing his recommended candidate and he is totally displeased and angry at my action. The following Monday morning, 20 personnel, directly from the Delhi CBI office raided my house, my office in Goa and also raided the houses of my mother and sister at Kochi. I was not allowed to call anybody during the time of the raid but at the end of the raid, when they could not find any incriminating documents either from my home or office, or any ill-gotten wealth or from the homes of my mother and sister at Kochi, perhaps the CBI knew they had climbed up the wrong tree. In fact, the Investigating Officer, Dy Superintendent of Police of CBI, one Mr NK Mukherjee, requested me to help find railway berth reservations in the coming days for his troupe to go back to Delhi. He told me that he had expected that the search would yield about ₹15-20 lakhs in cash in black money tucked away in some cells in my house as per some anonymous letters. Instead they got ₹4,500 along with the domestic account book of my wife which indicated the money withdrawn from the bank, expenses and the balance. They were informed that I was building a large mansion in Kochi, which was half built and asked me for the source of income. However, they did not know that I had sold my flat in Alaknanda in New Delhi at a price of ₹48 lakh, received in cheque which was put into my Capital Gain Account and I was spending from it. I also told them that I expected to complete the house at a cost of about ₹60 lakh, paying the balance from my Naval Service retirement benefits. The CBI was shocked when they knew the truth. They were fed with partially distorted informations.

My family had bought 4 pieces of land from Kesarwal Estate in Goa, all paid by my friend, late Commodore P Sachedev, eventually for the purpose of having a "Friendship Naval Colony". The pieces of land were bought in the name of my wife and two daughters initially but to be transferred later to our naval friends – all paid by cheque by Commodore Sachedev and accounted properly. Revealing this truth upset the CBI further as all their calculations had gone awry. They asked me how I was financing my elder daughter Nidhiya who had been studying for the past 8 years in Ivy League colleges in USA. I told them that she was on full scholarship from 1991 onwards and I did not have to spend a penny. I showed proof to that effect and the CBI did not know where to look further. They asked me whether I had any cardamom estate in Munnar and huge properties in the hilly station next to Kerala. I confirmed that I had a property without 'patta', bought 10 years ago when I was in Cochin, in 1990, in partnership with one Mr Mohammad Ali, a retired engineer from Kerala government, at a cost of ₹40,000. The registration documents were shown to them shared between two owners. They had been informed by anonymous letters that I have huge tracts of land in the hill station at Munnar, all bought with black money!

The CBI crew returned to Delhi the next day, but the Goa newspapers flashed the news in the usual manner, saying that various incriminating documents were taken into custody. That evening I called the Secretary (Defence Production), Mr Probir Sengupta, who showed his total surprise at the raid since as per government norms, his permission had to be sought before the raid by the CBI of any of the departments/ Public Sector Undertakings under him. There were a few Malayalee staff at the Defence Minister's office in New Delhi some of whom were friendly with me. On enquiring with them, I was informed that the Defence Minister, Mr George Fernandes personally called up the CBI Director and ordered the raid based on various letters received by him from Goa. Even the letters received directly by the Defence Minister's office were sent to the CBI office to substantiate the reason for the raid. Most of the letters were investigated by the Ministry of Defence and found that they had no substance. Mr George Fernandes knew it but the fact that I had not inducted his crony to the Shipyard enraged him no end and based on strings of allegations though false, he ordered the CBI raid without even consulting his Secretary (Defence Production). Very unusual indeed but that was the truth.

In the evening my mother and sister called me and told me of the raids in their houses. My sister was worried that all the gold of my married daughters – Nidhiya and Nayana, and that of my wife were kept in the Cochin locker of Nedungadi Bank (later became Punjab National Bank), could also be seized. After the raid as per practice, all my accounts in various banks in Bombay, Delhi, Goa and Cochin were frozen as per directions of CBI. As Naval officers, when moving from one station to another, we opened new bank accounts at the new place of posting and on moving to another place, tended to leave the accounts opened in the previous station but with meagre amounts. This is because when we get posted back again in the same station, we don't have to go through the formalities of starting a fresh bank account. The CBI also had frozen all the bank lockers at Goa. One locker had my wife's small amount of jewellery for immediate use which was not even accounted for by the CBI as the value was too negligible to account. The second locker at Goa after opening in 1995 was never used even once and when opened at the time of the raid, in 1999, was found empty. This locker was opened in 1995 just to satisfy the request of the State Bank of India's Branch Manager there, I recall. All these surprised the CBI and obviously they knew that they had been misled. Mr Mukherjee, the Investigating Officer and Deputy Superintendent of CBI, even told me that it is going to be an uphill task for the CBI to unwind the process – since raiding a Joint Secretary level Officer (Rear Admiral equivalent) can only be done by getting approvals from various levels and exonerating me just after the raid would mean that the CBI had failed in their investigations prior to conducting the raid. But fortunately for them and unfortunately for me, they got a useful lead. That was when my brother-in-law in Kochi, heard about the freezing of our bank accounts and lockers, asked me to send across to him by post the key of the Nedungadi Bank locker at Cochin, with an authority letter from me to enable him to remove all the jewellery from that locker. This was only to ensure that the CBI eventually will not seize that locker too and prevent my daughters and wife from getting their rightfully acquired jewellery. That was the good intention of my brother in law. On his words, I thought I will send across the keys (along with the authority letter) by hand of the Indian Airlines pilot from Goa to Cochin. So, I put the key of the locker with the authority letter in a sealed envelope and gave to my liaison officer at GSL, Mr Naik, to be handed over to the pilot of the Indian Airlines flight from Goa to Cochin. Thereafter, I had to urgently leave for Delhi to apprise the Secretary Defence Production of the developments. On reaching Delhi, my wife called me up and told me that my liaison officer brought the packet back, saying that the Captain of the Cochin flight did not accept it. I then asked my wife to tell my liaison officer, to send the packet to me in Delhi by air through the next available flight from Cochin. My intention was to send the packet to Cochin most urgently by post from Delhi or through someone going to Cochin. My liaison officer sent the parcel through the hand of a Pilot to Delhi as instructed by my wife. The Delhi Office sent a peon to collect the parcel at Delhi airport. He collected the parcel from the airport, came to Ashok Hotel where I was staying, called me from the Reception counter and I asked him to come up to my room to give the parcel. The bell rang and when I opened the door, Mr Mukherjee, the DSP along with 3 other CBI officers were there with him. They asked what was in the parcel and I said it is the key to the bank locker in Cochin along with some medicines for my mother which was put into the packet by my wife to be sent across to Cochin. Later I realized from the CBI Officers themselves, that when Mr Naik took the packet to the Goa airport, all my related movements were under the scanner by the CBI. I had sufficient enemies in Goa! After this incident I did not even trust my liaison officer. The CBI somehow or other knew that a key was being sent by air parcel to Delhi and they waited at the air parcel area in Delhi airport, coolly found out from the GSL Delhi Office who is going to collect the parcel and followed him right through to Ashok Hotel. It did really surprise me also. The CBI had immediately directed to seize the locker at Cochin and thought that the missing amount of ₹ 15 or 20 lakh in black money is indeed kept in that locker. They did not believe me when I told them that it was some old gold ornaments of my family members, acquired over a period of 30 years and kept in my locker. This episode made the CBI take a 'U-turn' and look at all related issues with a magnifying glass as they felt I had something to hide. Thus, the case they wanted to close after their raid at Goa was re-opened. I was asked to come to Cochin to enable opening of the locker in my presence. The opening of the locker revealed total gold worth ₹3.5 lakh, as assessed by the local Assessor appointed by the CBI. There was nothing else in the locker. This was the greatest surprise for CBI as they could not believe that between 3 Nair ladies following the matriarchal system in Kerala, where wealth is assessed by the amount of gold that one is holding, the value of total gold found in the locker was only amounted to ₹3.5 lakh.

While I was still in Goa Shipyard Ltd, the CBI asked me to render a detailed financial statement for the previous eight years (1991 – 1999) which was the "check period". The immovable properties possessed by me and my dependants, movable properties possessed by me and my dependants, statement of financial investments and cash possessed by me and my dependants, were to be detailed. On these details, the details of properties held under whose name, date of acquisition, mode of acquisition, name and address of person/s from whom acquired, price paid for the properties, source from which the payment was made, particulars of sanctions obtained from competent authorities if any, details of properties disposed of, held under whose name, date of disposal or sale, sale price, how was the proceedings utilized or invested, name and address of the person to whom the property was sold, were to be given. In the case of movable property, details of property such as gold ornaments, car, furniture, electronic items, etc held in whose name; date of acquisition; mode of acquisition, name and address of person/s from whom acquired and such other details, were to be given. With respect to statement of financial investments and cash possessed by me and my dependents, details of investments, held in whose name, date of investment, amount of investment, present value, source from which payment was made, name and address of bank or organization where investment has been put, details of sanctions obtained, etc were to be given. These details were to be given for the entire check period of 8 years – January 1991 to December 1998. This was one of the most difficult and harrowing task for me and my wife. It was indeed the patience of my wife and her memory of almost every purchase or investment that we had done during the past decade that helped us to put the facts and data together after an intense two months of self search – most difficult and frankly a self insulting task. It was done by my wife Promila – in her long hand, initially. Together my wife and I had to walk through our past memory lanes, day by day, to recall events, dive through old bank passbooks and bank statements including discussions with people, bankers and in a span of about 60 days we put the documents together. One or two pages of the documents are kept below. This is to indicate the depth of involvement required for compiling these voluminous data with utmost accuracy. This was the height of harassment by the CBI.

The CBI continued their investigations. I continued as the CMD of GSL for the rest of my full tenure of 9 months and retired with full retirement benefits from GSL. There was not even a departmental enquiry ordered by the Ministry of Defence, despite the CBI raid but the anger and disappointment lingered in the minds of my enemy groups in Goa very strongly. The expelled Manager of Delhi, Mr Sharma continued his spite against me and Cdr Shaikh on the platform of Mrs Vandana Jingan the ex-Steno of Delhi Office who had already migrated to the USA, after being expelled from GSL.

STATEMENT NO. III

Statement of movable property possessed by the undersigned and his dependents either in their own names or in the names of others as on 31.12.98 (Here I O has to give last date of period of check)

Details of property	Held in whose name	Date of acquisition	Mode of acquisition (whether acquired by purchase or inheritance on gift or any other means	Name & address of the person from whom acquired
(1)	(2)	(3)	(4)	(5)
1. Ornaments and jewellery (Full list including loose pieces of gold silver and precious stones and any other articles made therewith)				
2. All means of conveyance (Car scooter, motorcycle, moped, etc.)				
1. Ornaments comprehensive list attached. * ONLY 361.39 GMS BELONG TO MRS PROMILA MENON AS SHOWN IN ATTACHED LIST BALANCE IN LIST 2&3 OWNED BY MARRIED DAUGHTERS NOT DEPENDENTS AS IN LIST ATTACHED.	* Mrs.Promila Menon (see note below and lists attached of details)	Approximately 90% of the ornaments indicated in the attached list as belonging to Mrs.Promila Menon, received by her 28 years ago. Balance over a period of two decades.	90% received by wife as wedding gifts 28 years ago-others were purchased -exchanged - gifts from relatives-cannot be precisly recalled and identified.	Mrs.Mohana Nair, mother of Promila Menon,Mrs.A. Menon mother of Mr.B.R. Menon. Some purchased,exchanged , recd as gifts from relatives separate list attached.
2. 1983 Model Ambassador car. No.DL 2C - 8008	Mr.B.R. Menon	1992	By purchase	Through car dealers. (Second hand)

Price paid or if acquired otherwise than by purchase Its value at the time of acquisition.	Source from which payment was made for the property and mode of payment.	Particulars of sanction obtained or intimation given to competent authority in respect of acquisition.
(6)	(7)	(8)
1. Cannot recollect with certainty	From personal savings and earnings of Mrs.Promila Menon & Mr.B.R. Menon and some by exchange of old to new and some by inheritance and some by presentation.	Not considered necessary as it was mostly exchange or inherited Some purchases done at varied points in time in the past.
2. Rs.60,000/-	Loan from the Navy (Govt.)	________

Contd...

	(2)	(3)	(4)	(5)	(6)	(7)	(8)
3. Furniture							
List attached.	Mr.B.R. Menon & Mrs.Promila Menon	1995-99	Purchased	Director of Industry, Goa.	Rs.23,100/- + Rs.11,200/-	From savings by Cheque	not applicable.
Old sofa sette	- do -	1991	Purchased	Delhi Market.	Rs. 4,000/-	-do-	-do-
4. Carpets - 3	- do -	1982-83	- do -	London Market sales	Approximately £ 150	out of salary drawn in U.K.	
5. Radio, T.V., VCR, Tape recorder, typewriter, personal computer, etc.							
a) 1 Weston TV (Old)	-do-	1994	Purchased	Mumbai Market	Rs.12,000/-	savings	-do-
b) 1 V.C.P.	-do-	1992	- do -	Delhi Market	Rs. 1,000/-	-do-	-do-
6. Airconditioner, room/desert cooler, room heater, etc.							
1 TON Fabricated Air-Conditioner	-do-	1992	-do-	Delhi Market	Rs.12,000/-	-do-	-do-
7. Electrical gadgets such as geyser, washing machine, refrigerator, freezer, oven, micro overn, mixie, other kitchen gadgets etc.							
One Fridge	- do -	1988	-do-	Cochin Market	Rs. 8,000/-	-do-	-do-
Mixie (Kenwood)	- do -	1982-83	-do-	London Market	£ 50	-do-	-do-
8. Projector, camera, slide projector and other such articles.							
Camera (Minolta)	- do -	1988	-do-	Cochin	Rs. 1,500/-	-do-	-do-
9. Watches, pens, paintings and other valuable articles							
Normal Wall decoration paintings	- do -	1982-1992	-do-	From Delhi, Mumbai, Calcutta, London & Cochin.	Approximately Rs.73,000/-	-do-	-do-
10. Crockery, cutlery and other utensils							
Indian Crockery & Cutlery	- do -	1980	-do-	Delhi	Rs. 5,000/-	-	-
Imported crockery		1983	-do-	London market	£120		
11. Clothing and other personal articles							
Full sets of glassware	- do -	Over 25 years	-do-	Delhi, Bombay, London, Calcutta	Approximately Rs.10,000/-	-	-
12. Sewing machine							
13. Fire arm							

Contd...

	(2)	(3)	(4)	(5)	(6)	(7)	(8)
14. Animals							
A Pair of Boxers	- do -	Early '95. Own Bred.	-	-	-	-	-
15. Other articles.							
Cut Glasses	- do -	From Navy days From 1969-1998	-do-	-do-	Approximately Rs.25,000/-		

Signature ____________

Date ____________
Full Name ____________

Designation ____________

Address ____________

[illegible]ING TO PROMILA MENON

Sr. No.	ITEM	Nos.	Wt./Gms.	Wt./Sovereigns	SOURCES:
1.	Green stone necklace	1 No.	16	2	Given by Mrs.Nair –Mother of Mrs.Promila Menon
2.	Mauve Stone necklace	1 No.	44(22 gold)	3	– do –
3.a)	Dropping studs (green)	1 pair)			
b)	Dropping studs (mauve)	1 pair)	16.75	2.2	– do –
4.	Necklace (22 ct) with 1 sovereign each (green stones)	1 No.	70.9	8.5	– do –
5.	Necklace (22 ct) with 1 sovereign each (red stones)	1 No.	70.9	8.5	–do –
6.	Long chain with pendent	1 No.	20	2.5	– do –
7.a)	Red stone necklage	1 No.	14	2	– do –
b)	Ear ring	1 pair	8	1	– do –
c)	Finger-ring	1 No.	4	1/2	– do –
8.	Necklace with 1 single blue stone.	1 No.	20	2 1/2	Gift from aunt of Mr.Menon for wedding
9.	Plain gold earrings	1 pair	8	1	Given Mrs Nair Mother of Mrs.Promila Menon.
10.	Thick bangle	1 No.	16	2	Old bangle given and bought new at the time of her wedding.
11.	Lakshmi (silver coated)	1 No.	–	–	Presented to her by a friend from office.
12.	Coin (gold) Indian from MMTC.	1 No.	13	1.5	Bought during the 50th year of independence from MMTC.
13.	Pearls (cultured) necklace	1 No.	Rs.900/-		Bought from savings.
14.	Chain pearl (set)	1 No.	Rs.700 + Rs.500/-		– do –
15.	Ear-studs	1 pair	Rs.2,500/-		– do –
16.	Chain Earrings Rings.	1 3 2	10 3 10) 7)	3.5	Gift from Mrs.Nair –Mother of Mrs.Promila menon. – do – – do –
17.	Earrings	1 Pair	4	About 1/2	Bought from savings.
18.	Pearl earring	1 Pair	8	1	– do –
		Total:	361.39 Grams.		

ORNAMENTS BELONGING TO NIDHIYA-MARRIED DAUGHTER & IN [illegible] BANK, COCHIN –ACQUIRED OVER A PERIOD OF 25 YEARS.
IN THE CUSTODY OF MRS. PROMILA MENON.

Sr. No.	ITEM	Nos.	Wt./Gms.	Wt./Sovereigns.	GIFTS FROM: (Some of the ornaments have been exchanged as and when found necessary)
1.	Studs	1 Pair	6.3	1/2	Her uncle Lt.Col. Anil Nayar, 3 Guards, c/o.56A.P.O.
2.	Bangles	4 Nos.	63.9 gms	8	Her aunty Mrs.Anila, 'Saanam', Cheranaur Road Edappally, Ernakulam.
3.	Chain	1 No.	22.4	2.25	– do –
4.	Bangles ₹ 2 Ring 5 — 2	1 No.) 1 No.)	13.2	1.25	– do –
5.	Chain	1 No.	17.8	2.75	Her uncle Lt.Col.Anil Nair, 3 Guards, C/o.56 A.P.O.
6.	Earring	1 pair	4	1/2	– do –
7.	Bangles	6 Nos.	48	6	Her grand-mother – Mrs.A. Menon,Raniland, Edappally P.O., Cochin –24, Kerala.
8.	Earring (without pearl)	1 pair	11.8	1	Her mother Mrs.Promila Menon, Shipyard House, Airport Road, Chicalim, Goa.
9.	Necklace Studs	1 No. 1 pair	43 19.5	5 2.3	Her grandmother – Mrs.Mohana Nair(Mothers' mother) A 43 D.D.D.A. flats, Munirka, New Delhi-67.
10.	Sovereigns	10 Nos.	80	10	RECEIVED ON THE OCCASION OF WEDDING OF MRS.NIDHIYA MENON.
11.	Sovereign (Australian)	1 No.	8	1	————DO————
		TOTAL	337.1 GMS		

10

Challenging CBI After Retirement

Back at Cochin after my retirement in December 1999 from GSL, I found it difficult to make both ends meet since all our bank accounts were frozen. There was no case against me by the CBI, except an odd enquiry from here and there, asking for some more odd details regarding some of my financial investments, perhaps as a part of harassing the accused. Seven months into my retirement and 18 months after the raid, despite my writing many letters to the CBI Headquarters, they did not release my bank accounts and I therefore took up the case against the CBI at the High Court of Kerala, indicating the facts on the ground and that I am unable to survive since all my banks remained frozen. Perhaps this is the first time ever in the annals of CBI history that someone has taken up a case against the CBI, without the CBI even issuing a chargesheet. This infuriated them quite a bit that I had the audacity and boldness to challenge the CBI. The Hon'ble Justice Koshy who was the HC Judge, asked the CBI that it has been 18 months since the raid and I had retired with full benefits from GSL 9 months after the raid and now what is the reason that the CBI is hanging on to this investigation? The CBI replied, saying that they are still investigating. The Hon'ble Judge asked whether the accused is an NRI or a Uniformed Officer who served the Indian Navy for 30 odd years with distinction and has been Vigilance cleared by the CBI only in end 1994 when he was appointed as the CMD of GSL, as per the prevalent CVC norms of senior appointments. What was the further investigation they were doing? The Hon'ble Judge ordered that the investigation may be completed within the next 5 months and in the meanwhile, my Cochin bank accounts may be released. Thus, I got my Cochin bank accounts' released but CBI did not release the gold ornaments which was in my bank locker. By then the CBI had the measure of me and they knew that I may go for defamation against the CBI if they exonerate me after further investigation. They therefore cooked up a disproportionate assets case against me by inflating my expenses and assets and reducing my income for a check period of 8 years from January 1991 to December 1998 and registered a case in the

Goa Sessions Court against me for disproportionate assets of ₹37.4 lakh in a period of 8 years.

I crushed the CBI, disproving 72 prosecution witnesses in the Goa Sessions Court – fighting a lone battle with CBI for 13 long years during my retirement. That is the prime story of this book.

11

Legal Fight with CBI

After retirement when I had taken up the case in the High Court of Kerala and the High Court ordered to complete the investigation within 5 months, the CBI did not know where to begin and particularly to proceed further against me since there was no evidence till then (18 months after the raid) which they could gather to prosecute me. While cooking up a trumpeted case against me, they had to get the CVC's sanction. The CBI therefore approached the CVC to register a case against me before the date set by the Kerala HC for completion of investigations. The CVC then countered CBI that they had my detailed report – letter of 29th October 1999 given by me earlier, clearly indicating that I had a surplus of ₹ 10 odd lakhs during the check period clearly proving with exact expenses, income and assets – and asked them whether CBI had investigated all the aspects and evidence given in my report. This is the report that was handed over directly to the then CBI Director Mr RK Raghavan by Mr Ajit Doval – the then additional Director of IB – and present National Security Advisor, on my request. I had also handed over a copy of the letter with all 7 enclosures to the IO Mr Mukherjee in New Delhi through GSL Delhi Office. Of course I did not insist for a receipt for, I was not known then to the most treacherous and heinous way the CBI can stoop to save their skin. In fact, the CBI had not done any investigation on my report because if they had done honestly, they had to drop my case immediately then and there. After the refusal by CVC to allow to register a case against me without investigating the matters in my report by CBI, CBI realised they had to do an investigation somehow or the other. I was then called to Delhi for meeting with the Joint Director of CBI, Mr Upadhyay. When I went to Delhi to meet him, he told me that the Investigating Officer had received only my letter of 29th October 1999 and not the related enclosures! The crook IO Mr Mukherjee must have given this alibi to the CBI Joint Director Mr Upadhyay that the letter was handed over by me to the CBI Director Mr Raghavan in person without the enclosures. But of course I did not get a receipt either from CBI Director's office or from the IO's office when my most vital documents were handed over to their office. I just believed them. That was a great mistake committed by me. The Joint Director told me that he only now knows the claim by the IO Mr Mukherjee that my letter of 29th September 1999 reached him from the office of the CBI Director but there was no enclosure at all. The voluminous enclosures attached with the letter were missing. Obviously the IO was lying to escape any further rap on the matter from his senior officers for non-investigation by him. In the presence of the Joint Director, I gave an additional set of enclosures to the IO who gladly accepted it and I returned to Cochin. Here again I did not insist for a receipt. I understood from the CBI office then that the Joint Director Mr Upadhyay has gone immediately abroad on some small term assignments thereafter, and therefore I assume there was none senior enough who met me and knew my case to oversee the investigations being undertaken by the crook IO. This was an opportune moment for the IO to play his games. The IO must have done a shoddy investigation on the details submitted by me, reported his false findings to the CVC and quickly put up a trumped up case of disproportionate assets against me and registered a case against me – 15 days later after the 5 months time given by the HC of Kerala. I could have even challenged that. The CBI did not obey the HC and flouted the date given by the Court, but since I knew 100 per cent that all my transactions, investments and purchases were transparent and fully accounted for, I could easily call the bluff of the CBI. At that time, little did I realize that it will take me 13 long years to get myself acquitted from the clutches of the CBI? Of course the details gathered by me, item by item, during my check period of 8 years, which formed the fundamental basis of my letter to the CBI did help me immensely eventually in destroying 72 prosecution witnesses' statements along with the help of their own list of 80 documents which were part of the chargesheet. It must have taken a very clever manipulation by the IO – Deputy Superintendent of CBI, Mr NK Mukherjee to cook up a case and also prove to the CVC that despite my letter and enclosures given to the CBI, there is a need to prosecute me and the only way is to register a case and allowing the trial. The CBI had to do it to save their face.

Initially when all these data were sent to the CBI, they had nothing more to say. A copy of that letter, I had separately addressed to the Chief Vigilance Commissioner – Mr Vittal – and personally handed over to him along with the enclosures at his office in Delhi. All these were done while I was still the CMD of GSL to prove to the CBI that there were no expenses or investments which were not intimated to the CBI, and therefore they may cancel their investigation and drop the case but they did not do it. After my 5 year tenure, when the Navy and the Ministry of Defence moved papers for extension of my tenure in GSL in end 1990, 9 months after the raid, the CBI did not clear my case from the vigilance angle. The points to be noted here is that they had raided me in February 1999 and investigations were on for 9 more months, prior to my retirement in November 1999, nothing could be found wrong against me; not even a departmental enquiry could be instituted and yet the CBI did not clear me from the vigilance angle – a mandatory requirement prior to an extension of my tenure in GSL. Thus, I had to retire on 8th November 1999, with a CBI syndrome hanging around my neck but without any chargesheet against me till then.

When the chargesheet was issued on 15th November 2000 by CBI, I was the CMD of M/s TELK (Transformers and Electricals Limited, Kerala), a Public Sector Undertaking of the Kerala government. My lawyer, Advocate CC Thomas told me that without the sanction of the Kerala government, the CBI cannot register the case against me and therefore it is best to challenge the chargesheet itself filed in the Goa court. Accordingly I challenged the chargesheet saying that there was no sanction of the competent authority. The CBI contested that when the crime was committed I was CMD of GSL and since at the time of chargesheet I was a retired employee of GSL, there was no need for sanction from the Central Government. To this my lawyer argued that whatever may be the case, since I was Chairman of a Kerala government Public Sector Undertaking, the CBI should have taken sanction for prosecuting me, from the Kerala government. Having not done so, this amounted to wrong registration of the case which is bad in law and not permissible. The CBI produced some Supreme Court judgments wherein they had quoted an earlier instance of a Public Sector Senior Officer who moved from Public Sector to Public Sector trying to evade prosecution and therefore this being of similar nature – so felt the Supreme Court – the CBI could move against the accused without further sanction.

Having lost the case in the lower court, I moved the High Court of Goa. While discussing with my senior lawyers in the Goa HC, I realized that, most of the lawyers and even judges were rather disinclined to give a verdict against the CBI. Despite very strong arguments by my lawyers in the Goa HC, the HC agreed with the judgment of the lower court that in the peculiar circumstances of the case, sanction is not required to prosecute me. On the advice of my lawyer Advocate CC Thomas, I moved the Supreme Court on the matter.

Unfortunately, in those days, the Indian industrial scenario was filled with scams and allegations of corruption of Chief Executives of various industries.

Those had a salutary influence in the minds of the judges that corruption is rampant in the industries and they always tended towards a trial rather than acquittal due to lack of sanction. The Supreme Court, without even going through the merit of my case, said that if I am as innocent as I claim to be, then the trial will prove it and allowed the trial to begin.

This was after fighting the case for over a year at various courts in Goa and Supreme Court in Delhi and spending substantial sums of money from my retirement benefits. Finally, I had to submit to the Sessions Court in Goa for the trials.

Initially with the help of my Chartered Accountant in Goa Mr Robinson who was also a lawyer, I engaged another lawyer in Goa who was totally inadequate for the purpose. They just dragged the case for another year. I then went and met a renowned Bombay lawyer Late Advocate Lalit Chari known for his capability to handle CBI cases. I went to Bombay to discuss with him and after hearing my case he said two things: That by my going to the HC in Kerala against the CBI, the CBI was left with no other option but to prosecute me; otherwise their initial raid and conduct of the preliminary part of the case would come for harsh analysis by the superiors including the Ministries of Defence and Home and therefore one way or the other, the CBI had to chargesheet me which is what had happened. Had I not challenged the CBI in Kerala

HC in the first place, the investigation may have dragged on for a few more years and died a natural death as is the case in many instances. Now that the case has been chargesheeted against me despite all my efforts up to the Apex Court, I will have to go through the trial and he advised me to get in touch with Advocate Jose Peter D'Souza of Goa – a renowned criminal lawyer in Goa. It was the efforts and brilliance of Advocate Jose Peter D'Souza and ably assisted by his deputy Advocate Ms Caroline Collasso which helped me to get the acquittal in the Sessions Court in Goa on 30th April 2012, after a period of 13 long years of trial.

The letter dated 29th September 1999 by me to all and sundry, in no uncertain terms had established that I had a surplus over ₹10 lakh during the check period and not a deficit of ₹37 odd lakh as cooked up by the CBI. Neither the CBI Director, nor the Ministry of Defence nor the Chief Vigilance Commissioner, ever replied to me but must have taken cognizance of my letter. Hence there has been no further investigation or any enquiry conducted by anyone, till my retirement from GSL on 8th November 1999. I retired with full pensioner benefits and all other associated financial support available to CMDs of Public Sector in India.

The prologue to my case, submitted in the Court of Special Judge at Madgaon, Goa, by my Advocate Jose Peter D'Souza is given under:

"MAY IT PLEASE YOUR HONOUR

The accused above named begs to state and submit as under:

PROLOGUE

(a) The applicant joined the Indian Navy in October 1965. He served continuously till the day he prematurely retired in November, 1994 as a Rear Admiral with full retirement benefits including that of pension and provident fund. There was never an adverse remark against the accused during his entire tenure.

(b) While in service, since he was specifically handpicked by the Navy and the Central Government to streamline an otherwise militant and loss making Goa Shipyard Ltd, he retired prematurely from the Indian Navy and was appointed to the post of Chairman and Managing Director (CMD) of Goa Shipyard Ltd (GSL). To be noted is that prior to this appointment, the Accused had to be vigilance cleared, and was in fact done, by the Central Vigilance Commission (CVC), for which the Central Bureau of Investigation (CBI) plays the main role of investigating the concerned party. In this case the accused had been investigated into and cleared by the CBI itself till the date of his appointment ie 8th November 1994.

(c) Prior to his tenure as CMD of the GSL, the Company had been running into an annual loss on a regular basis. It was only under the control and direction of the Accused, that the GSL showed a profit for the first time to the extent of giving highest dividends to the Central Government. The relevant *Maritime International* magazine of May 1998 (page 27) was produced and marked as Exh 368.

The accused succeeded in improving discipline and increase productivity in GSL which took about 3 and half years to do so. These changes were brought about by the firm action of the accused in pulling up various concerned parties including Labour Union leaders. He brought in the Central Industrial Security Force (CISF), something which the GSL has been attempting to do for decades to prevent huge thefts, lawlessness and indiscipline in GSL. An article in the local daily *Herald* dated 28/1/2000 thus aptly described him as a "Redeemer of Goa Shipyard" and an 'unsung hero'. (Refer exhibit in 313 statements.) The accused along with his wife started Employees Assistance Programme in GSL to prevent alcohol addiction and helped many alcoholics in recovery. The then Chief Minister of Goa recognizing the accuser's "outstanding contribution to the growth of the Shipyard and to the growth of State of Goa" recommended him for the award of the Padma Shri. (Refer citation appended in 313 statements and marked as Exh 369 in his defence evidence.)

(d) However such firm action by the accused did not go well with the powers that be and corrupt Labour Unions that started to plot against the accused to have him out of the post. The Union leaders through anonymous letters sought to tarnish the image of CMD through trumped up malicious allegations. (Refers letters appended to 313 and Exh 370, 371. The accused was clearly a pawn in the machinations of the politicians as can be seen in the letter written to the Defence Minister by one MP against him and exhibited at 372, and another supporting him at Exh 373). Since he refused to bow down to pressure and corruption of some politicians who were well-connected, pressure was brought to implicate him in a false case of corruption. The CBI raided him in February 1999 and a case registered against him, yet he continued as CMD of GSL for 10 more months after the raid and retired on 7th November 1999 with full honours, receiving his entire pension due, gratuity and all retirement benefits. There was not even a departmental inquiry conducted against him.

(e) As a result of the raid however all his bank accounts as a rule were frozen since February 1999. The accused wrote numerous letters including a detailed statement (exhibit 109) explaining all queries on his income/assets/ expenditure to the CBI as demanded by them – but there was no chargesheet in sight even though 7 months had lapsed after their retirement.

(f) Having no other option, the accused filed a Petition against the CBI in the High Court of Kerala and vide Order dated 5/6/2000, while releasing his bank accounts in Keraia, the CBI was directed to complete the investigation expeditiously and in any event within five months from the date of order. (Refer judgment dated 5/6/2000 as appended to his statement u/s 313.)

(g) In retaliation and to save face, the CBI conducted a slipshod and one sided investigation and filed a trumped up case against the accused.

(h) Due to his impeccable credentials and reputation, even during the pendency of the present case, the accused was appointed as an Advisor to the Government of Kerala for the Development of Inland Waterways and minor ports and held the post of Chairman of Kerala Shipping and Inland Navigation Corporation Ltd, Kochi. The accused being Marine Engineer of great repute with a degree from Greenwich, UK was also Advisor Emeritus to Kunjali Marakkal School of Marine Engineering, Kochi. Presently he is holding the post of Maritime Advisor to the Union Territory of Lakshadweep as a Director of their board – appointed by the Central Government."

12

Concocting Evidences Most Dishonestly by CBI

I will now explain how the CBI has deliberately concocted my case in their favour. With respect to my house under construction at Thrikkakara, Kochi, I had actually spent ₹11,34,968 till the time of the raid in February 1999 and the amount was given through cheques in 4 instalments. But the CBI got the house examined by a CPWD Engineer, hired from Delhi who estimated arbitrarily the cost of construction till then at ₹19,69,965. The fallacy of this estimation was that he estimated three months after the check period when the case was registered, by which time substantial work had already been progressed. The CPWD Engineer could not also produce even the approved plan of the house. In the cross-examination, he admitted that there was no doors, windows, plastering, electric wiring or tiles for the floor, etc but the cost of construction quoted by him was for the entire unit of construction which should be completed in all respects as stated above. The Architect of the house Mr Ramesh Tharakan also admitted that the cost of the construction of the house till 31.12.1998 was around ₹11 lakh. The builder Mr Rajendra Kumar to whom the cheques were issued by me was not even examined by the prosecution, fearing that he might spill the beans.

Thus during the trial itself, it was proved that the CBI had deliberately inflated the asset value of the house under construction by ₹8,34,997. By conducting a shoddy investigation purposely and wilfully, accepting the wrong estimate of a CPWD Engineer who may have been prompted by the CBI to say what he admitted in the Court but without any evidence or proof. Also CBI deliberately did not examine the vital witness – the builder Mr Rajendran – who received the cheques. The court disallowed the asset value by ₹8,34,997.

The Architect's fee of ₹50,000 was paid by me beyond the check period, in the year 2000. The Architect Mr Ramesh Tharakan deposed to that fact in the court and there was no cross-examination of him by the prosecution. Therefore the expenditure indicated by the CBI of ₹55,000 as the Architect's fee paid by me was conclusively disapproved.

There were 4 plots of land bought in the names of my wife and daughters at Goa at a total cost of ₹9,37,962. In the long drawn out trial, through cross-examinations of all the various witnesses such as the owners of the plots, the managers of banks from where the cheques were issued from the account of Commodore (late) PS Sachedev, Mr Gundeep Sachedev, son of Commodore Sachedev and cross-examination of the Vigilance Officer of the Defence Ministry, Under-Secretary Mr AP Khathria (Defence Ministry), General Manager Personnel of GSL Mr Vajalu, it was proved beyond doubt that all the cheques for the property were issued from Commodore Sachedev's account and that the intention in purchasing the four pieces of land was to make a "Naval Officer's Colony" in Goa. After the demise of Commodore Sachedev, the properties which were bought initially in the names of my wife and daughters were returned to Commodore Sachedev's son, Mr Gundeep. That the CBI did not investigate at all the cheques for buying the lands in Goa were issued from Commodore Sachedev's account was seen as a clear sign of CBI deliberately hiding the truth from the Court, during the trial. At the end it was proved that since the total amount for the 4 plots having come from Commodore Sachedev's account, it was beyond any reasonable doubt that the purchases were in the nature of *Benami* transactions on behalf of

Commodore Sachedev. The entire amount of ₹9,37,962 was dropped from the list of my assets.

The gold ornaments which were found in the locker at Cochin, assessed by the Appraiser for ₹3,33,587 were proved to be old gold ornaments acquired before 1991 – the check period. The Appraiser could not prove during the cross-examination that they were new. In fact, during the cross-examination of my wife as a defence witness, it was stated that most of them were received by her as part of dowry at her wedding in 1971. The Court also found the value of the gold ornaments owned by the three ladies of a Nair family amounting only to a total of ₹3,33,587, clearly indicated that we as a family are not one of those gold lovers or hoarders and the meagre gold cannot be considered as assets acquired during the check period. ₹3,33,587 was therefore deducted from the list of my assets.

In order to prove that I had spent large amounts of money on internal and external air travels from Goa, the CBI went to some of the important travel agents in Vasco area, such as Gateway Travels, Mubeen Air Travels, etc and got details of travels conducted during my entire period in GSL – but the evidence collected by CBI and produced in the court was of all Menons of Goa who travelled! It was quite a hilarious document of proof produced by the CBI in the court indicating Menon's travel details such as Krishna

Menon, Govind Menon, Leela Menon and occasionally one Rear Admiral BR Menon VSM during a span of 5 years! It did not need much time for the court to realise the truth, but the defence lawyer had to cross examine all witnesses of the Travel Agents and to prove that there was hardly any travels pertaining to Rear Admiral BR Menon VSM and his family. At the end, about ₹3 lakh worth of bogus travel bills, submitted as my expenses, were disallowed by the Court.

My wife and I had gone to USA by Air India to attend my daughter's graduation ceremony in June 1994 and had paid return ticket fare of ₹1,10,000 by cheque from Grindlays Bank at Bombay. Despite my giving clear evidence, purposely the CBI did not believe these details and brought in Air India's Customer Relations Manager as a witness who estimated that the ordinary return full air fare of the travel route I had taken in June 1995 was ₹2 lakh approximately and he said that the travel route he had taken was Bombay-Geneva-London-Toronto-New York-Paris-Bombay. He said he had taken this route since the CBI has given him from my passport details of these ports of call wherein it was indicated that I had touched these cities. It took time to prove that I had not touched Paris (France) and that I had gone to Toronto (Canada), to see my uncle, from New York by road and not by air. The CBI deliberately did not investigate the Grindlays Bank cheque details at Mumbai given by me to Air India for the travel and stated that the payments were made by cash. A total lie by CBI. In the end the Court only admitted the cheque amount as my expenses and disallowed ₹90,000 from my expenses as indicated by CBI.

My second daughter Nayana's dental education at the Mangalore Dental College was pegged at ₹4 lakh odd by CBI. In arriving at this figure, they had added the returnable items such as Mess advance deposit, Hostel rent and charges for food in the hostel which were indicated separately by me as money paid from Nayana's personal bank account at Mangalore. To inflate my expenses, the CBI deliberately duplicated the expenses. All this took time to prove one by one and at the end it was proved that about ₹2.5 lakh was deliberately duplicated as my expenses by CBI and was disallowed by the Court.

For the wedding of my daughter Nayana at Mariya Park, Kochi, the cheques were paid by my mother and my sister sharing the ₹1 lakh odd expenses in early January 1998. Deliberately, the CBI included the expenses as spent directly by me and did not take into cognizance the cheques issued by my mother and my sister from their bank accounts and there was no investigations into that matter despite I demanding it. The court therefore reduced my expenses by about ₹1 lakh as it was proved that my mother and sister gifted this amount towards the marriage of my daughter.

There was an amount of ₹1,25,000 deposited by my wife in one M/s Aneja Group in Goa – a private financial group giving higher interest rates than the banks. This amount was the money earned by my wife during the check period, when she was working in Delhi. The CBI deliberately did not take into account the earnings of my wife despite valid proof but took ₹1,25,000 as her asset. After a long trial and examinations of witnesses and my wife and her employers, it was proved that my wife was working and had earned nearly ₹3.5 lakh from 1991 to 1993 in Delhi and this amount is only a part of the investment by my wife with the Aneja Group. The Court agreed with our view. The Court agreed to include my wife's salary of ₹3.5 lakh into my income, which was deliberately suppressed by the CBI.

When I was in Bombay, I had sold all my old but costly movable properties, such as, cut glasses, furniture, electronic and electric items and many such items acquired during my 30 years of service in the Indian Navy. This was in view of the fact that I was moving into a new job as Chairman and MD of Government Shipyard, to a fully furnished house including cutlery, crockery, electronic items, etc. I decided to sell my old artefacts in Bombay and got an income of ₹2.5 lakh from the sales. The CBI would not admit it despite my showing the advertisements in the records of the United Service Officers (USO) Club, Colaba, Bombay. At the end, I had to locate some customers such as Mr Fali Mehta of Bombay who bought some of my crystals and some of my naval friends who bought my golf sets, etc. They became my defence witnesses in Goa which gave credence to my statement about selling of old movable properties and the Court admitted the entire amount of ₹2.5 lakh as my income, despite the CBI's vehement denial.

I had bought a flat in Delhi in 1984 at Alaknanda through DDA and had rented it out since then. I sold the flat when I left Delhi to come to Bombay in 1994 after promotion as a Rear Admiral. During the period 1984-1994, the flat was rented out to many people. The rent was paid by all of my tenants, including the last, one Mr Ashok Rishi, directly to my Canara Bank account in Delhi. Mr Ashok Rishi had stayed in the flat for six years and had migrated to USA. It was strange that in the most abrasive manner, to suppress this, the IO Mr Mukherjee not only did not take into account the registered rental agreement signed by me with Mr Ashok Rishi but insisted that Mr Ashok Rishi should be brought in from USA as my defence witness to Delhi. He knew that it was impossible for me to get Mr Rishi to come to Delhi. Even Mr Rishi's direct payments to the bank were not accepted by the CBI.

Thus initially they denied my rental income amounting to about ₹2.5 lakh but interestingly, the IO had investigated the house tax paid by me to the CPWD office in Delhi and included ₹26,000 as the house tax paid as my expense for the entire period I was owning the house! After a period of long protracted trial, the Court admitted my claim of ₹2.5 lakh as my income in the check period.

We had two boxer dogs. We used to breed pups in Delhi and Goa and got two litters per year of 5 to 6 pups per litter. For a period of 8 years, we had indicated an income of nearly ₹2.5 lakh by selling pups. Despite giving proof and witness statements by veterinary surgeons both in Delhi and Goa and despite giving evidence of our Boxer winning the Best of Breed trophies, and original newspaper cuttings, both in Delhi and Goa, the CBI denied my income on this account. In the end, during the trial I had to bring the people who had bought the pups from me in Kochi and Goa as my witnesses and a Goa Veterinary Doctor to prove that they had indeed bought the pups from me at the price indicated by me. The income of ₹2.5 lakh was thus admitted.

In the Fixed Deposit incomes which were of my mother, Mrs PB Menon, my name was also added in lieu of my father, when he passed away in 1992. They were deliberately considered as my assets by the CBI. I had shown pass books after pass books, FD accounts after FD accounts, which began during my father's time far before the check period wherein my mother had included my name in place of my late father on his passing away in 1992. But the CBI deliberately would not agree. After a protracted trial, the Court agreed to my contention that ₹2.5 lakh are to be deducted from my assets since the sums were deposited before the check period, by my mother and father and belonged to my mother.

After I was raided and the CBI did not find anything incriminating, soon thereafter I went to Delhi and proved the facts to my superiors, such as Secretary (Defence Production), Joint Secretary (Shipyard) and narrated to them the incidents. They were all surprised at the CBI raid. I also then enquired with my Malayalee contacts in the Defence Minister's office and realized that it was the Defence Minister Mr George Fernandes who had, for more than one reason, actually directed the CBI to raid me with the hope of finding some serious incriminating evidence, based on which he could proceed against me. The various letters from Union leaders and MPs from Goa, alleging many irregularities in my running of the GSL, had sufficiently poisoned Mr George Fernandes's mind and made him believe that I was an undesirable element as CMD of GSL and should be removed. Despite many internal enquiries conducted at the Joint Secretary level from the Defence Ministry, having failed to find anything wrong, which made the Secretary (Defence Production) categorically state in writing to the Defence Minister that I could not be indicted at any cost, had annoyed George Fernandes further. He must have felt and hoped that a CBI raid would reveal the darker side of my administration. My not taking his recommended person from Ranchi into the books of GSL was the last straw in the camel's back. That action of mine made him take a vengeful decision to get me raided by the CBI.

When I was still CMD of GSL, many of my senior colleagues advised me to go and meet the CBI Director Mr RK Raghavan at Delhi and explain to him the truth. Thereupon I took an appointment from his office and went to meet him at 7 o'clock in the evening at the CBI Headquarters two months after the raid. He heard me with great patience all that I had to say and said that he will look at the reports of the Investigating Officer – Mr Mukherjee and will act accordingly. One thing he mentioned at the end really surprised me and indicated the bloated ego that was in his head. He said "Once I decide, that is final. There is nobody above me except God". I wanted to ask him was he not subservient to the Chief Vigilance Commissioner but I did not ask that question. Two years later, when CBI eventually chargesheeted me as a result of my going against the CBI in the High Court of Kerala, wherein the High

Court had ordered CBI either to exonerate me or to chargesheet me after 5 months of investigation, and when they chargesheeted me after a shoddy investigation I called Mr Raghavan on telephone at Delhi from my house at Kochi and asked him "Did you actually find disproportionate assets in my case as was indicated in the chargesheet, from the evidence collected?" He replied that the Court may relieve me if there is no sufficient evidence. I then asked him "if you feel that the Court may relieve me in view of insufficient evidence, why cannot you relieve me?", to which he answered: "You have gone to the High Court in your State against us and we are left with no choice but to chargesheet you." The entire story of this illegal case conspired up by the CBI against me, which made me go through a prolonged legal battle for 13 long years and my eventual acquittal for lack of evidence of my amassing any ill-gotten wealth, had been summed up in his two lines of reply, in the November 2000 telephone conversation between him and I, as narrated above.

When I was continuing as CMD of GSL after the CBI raid, the Investigating Officer Mr Mukherjee came to Goa for various investigations. He went to almost every bank and enquired whether I have any account in my name or in the name of my family members – *Benami* or otherwise; went to all travel agents to collect details of travels conducted by me which were eventually disproved in the Court, since I proved that travels by all Menons in Goa cannot be accounted to the travel account of BR Menon and his family. Mr Mukherjee even went to the Dandeli forest in Karnataka to check if I had bought wood from there for construction of my house in Kochi, in GSL's account, since CBI had been informed by the Union leaders that I along with the Senior Commercial Manager and wood technology experts had gone to Dandeli forest to buy good teak wood. It was true that we had gone to Dandeli forest but it was to procure suitable wood for building INS Tarangini, the first sailing ship of the Indian Navy for training purpose of naval cadets in India. All these ideas were injected into Mr Mukherjee's head – by these outside Union leaders, MPs and other disgruntled elements of the GSL clan, whom I had removed one by one during my tenure in GSL. They were all snakes in the Garden of Eden of GSL and it was my responsibility to weed them out one by one and make GSL a productive and efficient PSU and of course I did, but at what cost! It is these snakes who did their best to damage me and tarnish my image in the eyes of the Goan Society and at the various levels in the Defence Ministry.

Having not succeeded in finding anything more than what has already been revealed by me directly to the CBI, Mr Mukherjee in an attempt to trap me by luring me into bribery or to find out my mind – I do not know what was his real intention – came to my office at GSL at about 11 o'clock one day in August 1999 and met me. He had by then finished his investigations about me at Goa. He then told me that he had collected sufficient materials to put me in the dock in this disproportionate asset case. He further said that he would also have to give the clearance if the Ministry has to extend my tenure in GSL when my case comes up for Vigilance Clearance. With a smile on his poker face, he said that "all the above can be settled if I come to an understanding with him". I told him that I have nothing more to reveal than what I have already said and there is no further action I can take in any of these matters except to write a detailed letter to all and sundry, which I did later, on 29th September 1999. Then, Mr Mukherjee told me in chaste Hindi that he understood what I have said but please understand what he has said which will benefit him and me and I will have a peaceful retirement. I offered him a cup of tea and said I have nothing more to say and Mr Mukherjee departed with a sunken face. Till date I do not know what he had in his mind – an attempt to receive bribe from me or to indeed trap me.

I next met him in June 2000 in the office of the Joint Director (CBI) Mr Upadhyay. As a result of the directions of the High Court of Kerala, CBI after having decided to cook up a case of disproportionate assets against me to save their skin, they had to get clearance from the Chief Vigilance Commissioner and the CVC asked them whether they have investigated the detailed letter I had sent to them, a copy of which was personally handed by me over to Mr Vittal – the CVC – in Delhi. Perhaps the CBI never thought that CVC was fully in the picture and they would have to answer CVC on the matter and Mr Mukherjee did a volte-face and told the CVC that he could not investigate the case since he only got the letter and not the seven detailed enclosures attached to the letter. That was a blatant lie. The letter dated 29th September 1999 along with the enclosures were handed over to the CBI Director by Mr Ajit Doval who was the then Joint Director-IB (later became the Director-IB), and presently he is the National Security Advisor of the Modi Government. When I was called to Delhi and Mr Upadhyay (Joint Director, CBI) told me that they have not received the enclosure attached with my letter, I narrated the story in the presence of Mr Mukherjee and Mr Mukherjee immediately said that from the CBI Director's office there are lots of steps before it reaches the Investigating Officer's desk and it is likely that the enclosures have been misplaced. I said that the enclosures could not have been misplaced as they were tied together with the letter as one bundle. In any case I had carried a spare copy which I handed over to Mr Mukherjee in the presence of Mr Upadhyay, and he reluctantly received them. It was evident on his face that he had to undertake the investigations of these documents again. Fortunately for him the Joint Director was deputed abroad for 3 or 4 months and by the time he returned, Mr Mukherjee had cooked up the story against me, obviously without investigating the details given in the enclosures and filed a chargesheet against me. My job during the trial was therefore to explain the details of the enclosures which indicated with precise details and evidence of all of my income, assets and expenditure, showing a surplus of ₹ 10 lakh odd as against the CBI cooked up version of a deficit of ₹ 37 lakh over a period of 8 years from January 1991 to December 1998.

Couple of weeks before I was leaving Goa in December 1999 after my retirement from GSL, I met the MP from North Goa, Mr John Fernandez at a function. He came across to me and told me with a glee that he was instrumental in removing me from GSL. I turned around and told him that I was never removed from GSL but I finished my term after 5 years and completed my tenure. He was surprised and told me that his letter to the Defence Minister had therefore no effect. He then narrated that my former Manager of Delhi Office, Mr Sharma whom I had by then removed due to misappropriation of funds, had literally carried a letter from the Union leaders from Goa to be signed by the MP (Mr John Fernandez) for onward transmission to the CBI Director, Defence Minister, etc. Mr John Fernandez told me that he read the draft letter and told Mr Sharma, to get the letter typed. Mr Sharma got the letter typed, got MP's signature and handed over the same to the CBI Director and Defence Minister etc at Delhi. I recall that this letter was eventually referred to me by the Defence Ministry and I had to spend large amount of my time and effort in replying item by item refuting the charges with proof. As I said earlier elsewhere, large amount of my precious time during the last 2 years of tenure at GSL was spent on defending myself against extremely cleverly schemed letters by my enemies to hoodwink the Defence Minister and the investigating agencies.

Well apart from the frustrations and shame of the raid by the investigating agencies which were flashed across all National and local dailies, what my wife and I faced thereafter was a kind of ostracism in the social circles of Goa. I considered this as the most deplorable situation that we faced in Goa after the raid. That, it was an intentionally conducted raid, engineered by the Trade Union Defence Minister Mr George Fernandes mostly to appease to his rank and file was a fact, but this had no takers in Goa. I was

one of the top VIPs in the List of Precedence for various official functions and except the Governor of Goa – Lt-Gen Jacob (Retd) – former hero of the Bangladesh War and the Chief Minister of Goa – Mr Pratap Singh Rane, towards the end, the rest of the officialdom were viewing me with a natural suspicion after the raid by the CBI. There inborne suspicion could not be wiped away by our innocent smiles and no length of self explanation. We were always invited to most of the social functions as guest in view of our standing in the Society during the rest of our time in Goa, nearly 9 months or so after the raid – but the stigma stuck.

Slowly but surely the stigma got eroded in the minds of the people since nothing happened to me, no enquiry, no suspension or anything that normally follows a CBI raid and by the time we were leaving, most of the Goan people were of the view that it was a false raid engineered by those who were inimical to my revival plans of the Goa Shipyard. In fact, the Goan people were witness to the utter anarchy of the Shipyard 5 years ago and they knew for certain that discipline and the rule of law had come to stay and they knew who was responsible for it. Even the papers like *The Navhind Times*, on my departure from GSL carried captions such as "CBI raided CMD goes scot-free but the cloud follow".

At the send off party which was given by the Shipyard, at which most of the editors of newspapers were invited, I asked the *The Navhind Times* editor "why did you put even on the last day such a nasty headline on my retirement?", he quickly said, "I did not do it, some reporter must have done it, I will ask him for an explanation." All these were injected to the newspaper reporters by political factions of Goa and ousted Union leaders who were most prejudicial towards me for what cleansing I did in Goa Shipyard, which was their fiefdom before my arrival.

The then opposition leader in the Goa Assembly – Mr Manohar Parrikar – the present CM of Goa – was the only exception who perhaps understood fully what good I was doing for GSL and what I am going through. He was a friend and a good advisor to me during my difficult days in Goa. Being an Engineer himself and an honest person, he perhaps understood my difficulties better than most. Mr Parrikar knew that I was not fighting against any political faction or government, but trying to put discipline and order in an otherwise indisciplined Shipyard. He was happy I was reforming the Yard.

It is a known fact that sensationalizing the news, through a distorted twist is the hall mark of today's news publishers. Two months after my retirement, the *Herald* for a change put a decent heading and

10 HERALD, PANJIM, FRIDAY, JANUARY 28, 2000

addressing Con[illegible] meeting of Pond[illegible] workers held in [illegible]pany's mass co[illegible]

[illegible] participated in [illegible] petitive items [illegible] advisor of Uttra[illegible] participated [illegible]tition (extempo[illegible]

Menon: the redeemer of Goa Shipyard

After a turbulent tenure of five years, Admiral Menon retired as chairman and MD of the biggest industry of Goa — Goa Shipyard Limited. That he could have had a most peaceful and pleasant tenure as most other CEO's of our multitudes of PSEs, had he bowed most willingly to the pulls and pressures of the militant unions and self-centered politics of Goa is rather not known to many. Menon was a different kettle of fish. He was quick to realise two things on his ass[illegible]ption as the CMD towards the end of 1994. (a) The shipyard is in the grip of militant union faction, and unable to enforce any kind of industrial discipline — an essential ingredient for a structured growth of any industry in India. (b) The productivity of the company as claimed by the workers and as assessed by the management was from reality — far too low than expected which did not permit them to get the productivity incentive as was received earlier.

With unprecedented courage and determination Admiral Menon brought in CISF (Central Industrial Security Force) which successive previous CEO's of GSL failed to bring in by caving into the union pressure — since the union knew pretty well that the existing senario of the officers of company remaining as "captive" group of the militant faction will disappear in the event of induction of CISF —and that the law of the land will prevail. Also CISF will stop the petty theft from the property, thus stopping the [illegible] of PSE as a regular unchecked affair.

The entire work-force resisted the induction of CISF with all their might but Menon stood resolute that he withstood singularly and singly the pressures from within and from outside - both local and centre.

Menon demonstrated to the public and sundry how to break a strike based on unreasonable demands, with uncanny strength of mind and courage. Industrial discipline has come to stay in GSL forever. The rule of the land prevails - the jungle raj of yesteryears of GSL has become a thing of the past. Officers enforce discipline in the company. The independent smaller groups of unions now have their say - Multiplicity of unions in bargaining councils have come to stay.

Menon permitted plurality of minds of his own workers by disciplining workers - perhaps the fact not fully understood by the workers is of his contribution to democracy inside the yard was for their benefit alone. Understanding the militant forceful union marked Menon as their enemy number one. Their sole aim after the induction of CISF was to have him out, at any cost.

To this end, all whom he disciplined - those officers who were dismissed by him in GSL Delhi office and in Goa and the punished militant unions - all joined hands with a singular aim of "remove Menon" agenda. And in line with what is happening in our nation today, they found the easiest way is to tarnish his image and prove him corrupt through a series of allegations.

In the meanwhile GSL progressed, hitting national headlines by becoming the only shipyard in India to have exported ships, to have achieved very high profits thereby giving very high dividend to the shareholders and by producing high-tech warships for the Indian navy and Coast Guard with collaborative ventures with leading yards of Israel and Portugal. GSL also became the first indigenous shipyard to have made "Marine Cranes" for Indian ports - something which was imported hitherto.

Thus while disciplining the work-force, Menon with his vision and dynamism brought in technology too and converted the old Portuguese barge-building yard into a frontline warship building shipyard of recognition and repute!! The ten odd high-tech warships delivered by GSL during the five years of his tenure is a resounding testimony to his professional achievement for the country.

But all the achievements were of little consequence to those who were gunning for him. It is during mid-1997 the management realised that the so-called profitability is from sources other than "production" — the key to growth. "Production" by any measure of standards were not upto the mark - may be equivalent to the national industrial average - but certainly not up the mark of a self-respecting company according to Menon. He stopped the generous toll of Productivity Linked Incentive (PLI) which were given annually to the workers — whether they produced or not.

The most difficult education to a worker is to communicate to him that he is not producing or not producing enough.

Managements have never been able to communicate this naked fact and as a result industries have collapsed not able to take the burden of non-producing workers for too long. Again with profound strength of conviction and courage, Menon withstood stoically another bout of two months of total strike for non-payment of PLI. Most painful though the message was very clear to the workers. "You get what you produce. There is going to be no free lunches anymore".

This was not only a message clear as crystal to GSL but also to all the industries in Goa. What Admiral Menon has achieved by such actions to the industries in Goa, is not a fact understood in its required depth by the state. The workers returned to work — losing their two months pay — and productivity picked up slowly.

Withstanding internal and external pressures on such crucial nationalists issues, mo[illegible] diplomatically but courageously Menon has become a torch-bearer to many not only in Goa but outside the State also. But all these actions instigated those whose daily bread was curtailed by Menon's strong actions!!

They tirelessly tried for his eviction from the chair by baseless allegations. And eventually Admiral Menon became a victim of raid by the investigating agencies. That he remained in the chair for 10 more months after the said search and completed his full tenure is the proof to his integrity and credentials and a testimony that his investigators have not been able to make a case as yet.

The investigating agencies and their masters should have better wisdom to see through the glass [illegible] those who want to destroy the very fabric of the institution - and instead try and help and support those who have toiled to keep the nation alive with all their might and reputation.

"We are all the small pillars of our society. We cannot collapse under any pressure and if we do, the whole nation will collapse," Menon often used to say. And, he stood by his conviction.

"I am happy to leave GSL as I have done what I setforth to do in five years - GSL stands reformed in more ways than one and the reforms achieved at great cost to all in GSL are irreversible. This will help not only GSL but all industries in the future," said Admiral Menon.

He is leaving Goa as an unsung hero but he will be gratefully remembered for what he did.

In a growing industrial scenario, it is for Goans to realise and retain such talent as of Menon for the growth of the State's industries: for such talents are hard to find by in our nation.

(BY HTR)

acclaimed me publicly as the "Redeemer of Goa Shipyard Ltd".

The Goa Shipyard grew from strength to strength and it became the first Shipyard in India to export a ship – an ocean going tug to the Republic of Male in 1998. Amongst the public sector shipyards, GSL had also paid the highest Dividend (profit) back to the Central Government and I had the privilege to give a cheque for a wafty sum to the then Defence Minister Mr Mulayam Singh Yadav. Internationally also, my strong administration in GSL was acclaimed as one of the best. I had indeed run a Tight Ship. The Transfer of Technology from Israel to make the High Speed Aluminium Vessels called 'Super Dvora' gave a quantum jump to the ship building sector of the Yard. E-governance, total computerization, revolutionary changes of historic Union leadership from outside to Union leaders acceptable only from the employees of the Shipyard, induction of CISF, institution of time cards, salary linked punching attendance cards, breath analysers, etc brought in the desired levels of discipline and improved productivity tremendously. But all this were at the highest cost of the personal life of me and my wife.

The disgruntled elements and those who were gunning for my removal had dirtied the Goan ambience against me. Renowned lawyers like Advocate Peter D'Souza, Mrs Caroline Collasso had a difficult

time convincing the Court about my innocence since the judges who were basically Goans had heard a lot about my disreputation through the media and social circles and had therefore formed an opinion in their minds about me – quite natural and humane – in the circumstances described. In fact, during the Court appearances, Judge Mrs Nutan Sardesai used to treat me harshly, not even allowing me to put my hands on the front railings and demanding me to stand erect and not lean on anything. And my lawyer Advocate D'Souza had the boldness and strength of mind to publicly remonstrate to the judge Mrs Nutan Sardesai for showing such disrespect to me, a retired Admiral of the Indian Navy, in comparison to the respect and leniency she showed to other prosecution witnesses. Thereafter, she stopped going out of the way to show disrespect to me. What is important to know is that they all had formed an opinion about me before the trial, thanks to misrepresentation through the media for years.

Many of the defence witnesses of whom I only had very few like some of the bank managers and the veterinary doctor of Goa, were hesitant to come and depose in the Court against the CBI. I had 5 or 6 judges in a period of 12 years who heard the case during my trial and making their notings and it was a task far beyond the call of duty for my illustrious and good lawyers to explain and prove to each of them my case in totality and the proceedings of the trial till that stage. I consider it my good fortune that the last judge, Mrs Anuja Prabhudesai, Special Judge, South Goa, who took over my case during the final 7 months of the trial, had only the evidence from the witnesses in the file to study the case and the final arguments both by the prosecution and defence lawyers, to decide the verdict. The judgment makes an excellent reading fully reflecting her depth of understanding of each and every account inflicted and depleted by the CBI, to prevent my acquittal. The judge saw through the cooked up stories of the CBI and she relied entirely on the evidence and found that indeed I had a surplus of ₹9 lakh odd as against the deficit of ₹37 lakh cooked up by the CBI. Indeed it had fully supported my 29th September 1999 letter to all concerned which had all the honest ingredients of my financial status but the CBI refused to look at it and investigate with the desired degree of honesty. If they had, their case would have fallen through and they would have not been able to proceed legally against me.

During the various strike periods, I and my wife went through tremendous mental agony as a result of the misinformation spread by the disgruntled elements in Vasco. There was a time when the fisherwomen in the Vasco market refused to sell fish to my wife, pointing out "she is the Chairman's wife. Don't sell fish to her." The strike had affected the financial status of the workers families but little did the people realize that it was a self imposed strike directed by the outside Union leaders and was not something which I as Chairman had imposed. The outside Union leaders and their masters knew that they cannot have the Shipyard as their playing field to play dirty politics and indulge in pilferage of State owned materials; workers could not do any more while away their time that discipline has come to stay in GSL after the arrival of CISF and this fact something they could not swallow.

Many a time there were black flag demonstrations against me and the gates of the Shipyard were blocked by the striking workforce, shouting indecent slogans against me when I entered the Shipyard in the morning and left the Yard in the evening. Because of the strike, workers could not enter the Shipyard.

There were days when I used to go alone or with my wife at times, and go far away to the beach and sit and ponder on the extreme situation developing in the Shipyard. I had to stick on to my principles with great resolve and continue to do all I could to break the strike – which ultimately I did. The best part of the whole game was that when the striking workers and their leaders were approached by anybody who matter and asked for the reason for the strike, they really had nothing to say. There was no grievance, the Management never told them not to enter the Shipyard and work but it was on their own accord that they stayed away from work and a point in time came when they and their families may have asked this question themselves as to why they are striking. But having fallen prey to the instructions and demands of the outside Union leaders, it was difficult for them to swallow their pride and walk back to work. The Goans whatever may be their status or position, has an ego disproportionately larger than life. I realised it too late. This is the prime reason why the strike got prolonged till the local merchants and shops stopped giving groceries and provisions on credit and hunger and lack of daily necessities got the better of them. In the meanwhile the political leaders, including the Defence Minister, continued their best efforts to oust me from GSL through all possible means but without any success. All these while I had to continue the fight both within and outside.

The former Manager of GSL Delhi Office, Mr Sharma tried his level best to use Mrs Vandana Jingan's dismissal from the company as a tool to tarnish my image in the eyes of the Minister and also in the Shipyard. Dirty wall posters were stuck inside the Shipyard, showing me and the lady stenographer in compromising postures. Similar pictures were sent to the Ministry people as well, most of them engineered by the disgruntled elements. However, much of these may be considered as frivolous by senior officials but, this had a salutary influence in the minds of the uneducated workmen in particular and the Goan gentry in general regarding the truth of the matters. Of course it had tremendous demoralising effect on me no doubt which was the aim of those who indulged in this dirty practices. I am glad that I was not smothered under the onslaught of relentless efforts from many directions for years to demean and demoralize me. Nothing fortunately distracted me from my National duty of resurrecting and disciplining the Shipyard. But, for this my wife and I had to pay a very heavy price; it had ruined our personal life and our reputation when we were in Goa and later, the fight against the CBI for 13 years after my retirement that took away peace of my mind and that of my family, to a large extent. Nonetheless, I was happy with the ultimate result. GSL today is a trouble-free, well-run and motivated Shipyard, the heavy price that I paid for achieving this, notwithstanding. To indicate the degree of foul play by CBI in my case, I am giving below a gist of the chargesheet given by CBI to me on 15th November 2000 and the last para of the final judgement of the Special Judge Mrs Anuja Prabhudesai on 30 April 2012 completely exonerating me after 13 years of protracted trial.

I am indicating below the details of the CHARGESHEET and later the JUDGEMENT. That will highlight the nasty game plan of the CBI.

13

Chargesheet Filed by CBI

"Investigation has disclosed that accused Rear Admiral BR Menon (Retd) VSM had income from all the known sources to the tune of ₹63,33,067.17 during the check period from 01.14.91 to 31.12.98 as per Annexure I.

Investigation has further disclosed that accused Rear Admiral BR Menon (Retd) VSM had incurred expenditure during the said check period to the tune of ₹22,02,065.60 as per details mentioned in Annexure II.

Investigation has disclosed that the accused Rear Admiral BR Menon (Retd) VSM acquired assets during the said check period either in his own name or in the name of his wife Smt Promila Menon alias Smt Girija Menon or in the name of his two daughters, namely, Miss Nayana Menon and Miss Nidhiya Menon to the tune of ₹78,64,249.11, details of which are mentioned in Annexure III.

Thus, during the check period from 01.1.91 to 31.12.98, Rear Admiral BR Menon (Retd) VSM had

(i) Income of	₹63,33,067.17
(ii) Expenditure of	₹22,02,065.60
(iii) Assets of	₹78,64,249.11
(iv) Disproportionate Assets of	₹37,33,247.54

Disproportionate Assets have been calculated as under:

Expenditure + Assets – Income = Disproportionate Assets

Expenditure	₹22,02,065.60
+ Assets	₹78,64,249.11
	₹1,00,66,314.71
– Income	₹63,33,067.17

Thus, the Disproportionate Assets come to ₹37,33,247.54.

Investigation has disclosed that accused Rear Admiral BR Menon (Retd) VSM was found in possession of assets to the tune of ₹37,33,247.54 during the check period from 01.1.91 to 31.12.98 which are disproportionate to his known sources of income and for which he could not explain satisfactorily.

The aforesaid facts disclose commission of offence punishable under Section 13(2) r/w 13(1)(e) of Prevention of Corruption Act, 1988.

Rear Admiral BR Menon (Retd) VSM was not arrested during Investigation.

Since he has already retired from service, sanction u/s 19(1)(c) of Prevention of Corruption Act 1988 for his prosecution is not required.

(NK MUKHERJEE)
Dy Supdt of Police
ACU(1): CBI: New Delhi"

Before I explain the acquittal judgement, I am quoting some interesting facts of the case as brought out by the judge in her 89 page judgement, which will indicate the shoddy, distorted and one sided investigation deliberately done by the CBI to favour their case. Their game was to deliberately inflate my expenditure and assets and reduce my income during the check period – in my case 1991-1998 (8 years) – and establish a disproportionate assets case. In 72 sittings by 4 different judges, I disproved the CBI's case in totality.

14

Income-Related Issues

Quoting from the Judgement

Income from Salary of Wife

Learned Advocate Shri JP D'Souza has argued that the prosecution has not considered the income of ₹ 1,46,515, being the salary of his wife while she was employed from 1991 till 1995 with M/s Maheshwari Associates in New Delhi. Learned PP Shri J Vaz has argued that the certificate issued by Dw6 is undated and all these facts amply prove that the defence raised is only an afterthought.

It may be mentioned that the accused has deposed that his wife was working with M/s Maheshwari Associates as an Executive Assistant. The accused has produced the extract of ledger at Exh 349. The accused had also informed the CBI about the said fact. He has deposited that she had received total amount of ₹ 1,46,515 as certified by the owners of the company. He has produced the certificate issued by the said Company giving the said details along with the certified extract of their ledger, which are at Exh 349 collectively. The accused has deposed that he had informed the said matter to the Investigating Officer and had also written to the Joint Director of CBI on 11.7.2000. He has produced the said letter along with the postal receipt and the AD card, which are at Exh 350 collectively. He has deposed that the CBI has not taken into account the earnings of his wife.

The accused has also examined Dw6 Purushothaman Maheshwari. He has deposed that Maheshwari Associates is an Agency House, having their office at 411, Mansarovar, 90 Nehru Place, New Delhi. He has deposed that Promila Menon, wife of the accused, was employed with M/s Maheshwari Associates for the period from 1990 to June 1993 and that she was recruited through a recruitment agency. He has deposed that they had advertised the said post and the placement agency had provided them with the bio-data of Promila Menon and she was selected amongst the other applicants. He has deposed that the placement service agency had given their bill for ₹ 4,000. He has stated that the total salary paid to Promila Menon amounts to ₹ 1,46,515. He has confirmed the contents of the Certificate at Exh 349 collectively. He has stated to the CBI all the employment details along with the copies of the documents. In his cross-examination, he has stated that the balance sheet shows the salaries paid to all the staff including Promila Menon was paid salary of ₹4,500 which was subsequently increased to ₹5,000. He has stated that he is unable to produce the balance sheet because the records of 20 years old might have been destroyed. He has further stated that Maheshwari Associates is proprietorship concern and it is registered with the Sales Tax Authority and also under Shops and Establishment Act. He has denied the suggestion that Promila Menon was not working for his company from 1990 to June 1993 and that she was not paid ₹1,46,540.

The accused has also examined his wife Dw7 Promila Menon. This witness has deposed that the accused, ie her husband was posted in Delhi from 1990 to 1993. She has deposed that during this period, she was working with M/s Maheshwari Associates as Executive. She has deposed that she was initially paid salary of ₹4,500 per month which was subsequently increased to ₹5,000 per month.

The evidence of the accused Dw1 Balakrishnan Menon, his wife Dw7 Promila Menon and Dw6 Purushothaman Maheshwari vis-a-vis the document at Exh 349 produced by them amply proves that the wife of the accused, ie Promila Menon was working as Executive Assistant with M/s Maheshwari Associates from 1990 to June 1993 and that during this period she was paid ₹1,46,515. The documents at Exh 349 proves that for the month of November 1990 to March 1991 Promila Menon was paid ₹21,185 at the rate of ₹4,500 per month. The total income paid to Promila Menon from November 1990 to June 1993 was ₹1,46,515. Since this income include the salary of two months, ie November 1990 and December 1990 which was prior to the check period, an amount of ₹9,000 needs to be deduced and on deducting the said amount, salary paid to Promila Menon works out to ₹1,37,515.

It is to be noted that the Investigating Officer Pw51 Shri NK Mukherjee has admitted in his cross-examination that the wife of the accused was working as Executive Assistant with M/s Maheshwari Associates. He has however claimed that she had not earned any income from the said M/s Maheshwari Associates during the check period. He has stated that he does not remember whether he had recorded statements of the Directors, Officers or employees of M/s Maheshwari Associates or whether they had interrogated anyone from M/s Maheshwari Associates or whether they had verified the salary Register of M/s Maheshwari Associates. In the absence of such investigation or interrogation, it is not known as to on what basis the Investigating Officer has concluded that the wife of the accused had not earned any income from M/s Maheshwari Associates during the check period. The Investigating Officer has also not assigned any reason for Promila Menon to work for M/s Maheshwari Associates without any emoluments or salary. In the absence of such evidence, it is difficult to believe the statement of the Investigating Officer that said Promila Menon had not received any salary from M/s Maheshwari Associates. This being the case, there is no reason to reject the claim of the accused that during the check period Promila Menon had earned salary of ₹1,37,515 and in my view, this claim must be added to his income during the check period.

Income from Sale of Personal Artefacts

Learned Advocate Shri JP D'Souza has argued that the accused had derived an income of ₹2,25,000 from sale of personal articles and that the accused had disclosed the details of the transactions to CBI officers despite which the said income has not been included. As against this, learned PP Shri J Vaz has argued that the accused has not produced any documents to prove advertisement of sale or such articles and as such, the said claim cannot be considered.

At the outset, it may be mentioned that the accused is not required to prove his defence beyond reasonable doubt. All that the Court is required to see is whether the accused has been able to prove his claim by preponderance of probabilities. Now coming to the second claim, the accused has assignment abroad and also during his tenure in Indian Navy. He has stated that the list of the said items including the names and addresses of the purchasers are reflected in the statement at Exh 109 which was submitted to the CBI. He has further stated that the artefacts such as TV, golf sets, cut glasses, ACs, carpets and other electronic goods, which are listed in the statement at Exh 109 were purchased prior to the check period and sold before he joined GSL as CMD. He has stated that the total value of the items sold by him was ₹2,25,000 during the check period and that the CBI has not included the same in his income despite his intimation vide letter dated 28.9.1999.

The accused has also examined Dw4 Fali B Mehta. He has deposed that in the month of September 1994, he had visited United Services Officers' Club at Colaba, Mumbai and that he had seen one advertisement displayed in the notice-board stating that some household items were for sale at the house of Admiral Mr Menon. He has stated that full name and address of said Mr Menon was mentioned in the said advertisement. He has deposed that he went to the house of accused and found that several items such as refrigerators, cameras, air conditioners and crystal items were for sale. He has deposed that he was to celebrate his wedding anniversary and such, he and his wife had purchased some crystal items in order to gift the same to the family members and that he had paid cash of ₹30,000 for the same. In his cross-examination, he has stated that he had received intimation in writing from CBI officer to attend the office at Mumbai and that he was interrogated by CBI Officer.

It is to be noted that the prosecution witness Pw19 AP Khathria has deposed that he was Under-Secretary (Vigilance) since May 1994 and thereafter as Deputy Secretary in the Department of Vigilance in the Ministry of Defence, New Delhi. He has stated that as per the rules in force, every government servant is required to file a statement of the properties acquired and disposed of every year. He has stated that as per his letter dated 14.9.1999, he had supplied to the CBI the details furnished by the accused regarding purchase and sale of movable and immovable properties. He has produced the said statement which is at Exh 109. He has stated that statement number 4 pertains to the movable properties for the period ending 31.12.1998. It may be mentioned here that the statement number 4 at Exh 109 collectively pertains to the movable properties possessed and disposed of by the accused and his dependants between 1.1.1991 and 31.12.1998. The said statement indicates that the crystals which were held in the name of his wife Promila Menon were sold to Fali Mehta. The said statement also shows that the accused had also sold furniture, carpet, radio, electronic typewriter, firearm, etc to several other persons whose names are disclosed in the said statement. It is to be noted that through it was suggested to Dw4 that he was not called to the CBI Office and that the CBI officer had not recorded his statement, the Investigating Officer Pw51 has admitted in his cross-examination that he had recorded the statements of the persons whose names are reflected in the statement number 4, for sale of various items listed therein. The Investigating Officer Pw51 has stated that he had not relied upon the said statements as they do not pertain to the transactions during the check period. As stated earlier, evidence of Dw4 Fali Mehta amply prove that the accused had sold the said artefacts in the month of September 1994, which was during the check period. Though the Investigating Officer had recorded the statements of witnesses, he had suppressed the best evidence, which in my view, could have certainly thrown light on the date of purchase of the items and this warrants drawing of adverse inference. Under these circumstances, I do not find any valid reason to disbelieve the case of the accused that he had derived income of ₹2,25,000 from the sale of artefacts and this ought to be credited to the income of the accused.

Income from Lease of Flat in Delhi

Learned Advocate Shri JP D'Souza has argued that the accused had derived an income of ₹2,49,716 from lease of flat in Alaknanda, New Delhi. Learned Advocate JP D'Souza has argued that the accused disclosed the details of the lease to CBI Officers despite which the said income has not been included. Learned PP Shri J Vaz has argued that the initial agreement was fraudulent and the accused has no given reasons for not executing a fresh agreement or extending the lease in writing.

The case of the accused is that he owned a flat in Alaknanda, New Delhi. He has stated that he had leased the said flat to one Ashok Rishi and his wife Anu Rishi by executing registered Lease Agreement dated 3.11.1993. He has stated that the rent payable was ₹7,000 per month. He has produced the Lease Agreement at Exh 353 collectively. He has stated that the Lease period was from 3.11.1993 for a period of two years and thereafter the Rishi couple continued staying in his flat till February 1997. He has deposed that after adjusting the advance, the Rishi couple was crediting an amount of ₹5,550 per month for the period from 10th November 1993 till 21st February 1997. He has stated that the first payment made by Rishi couple was for ₹47,250 which was to be adjusted. He has produced the passbook of Canara Bank account held jointly by him and his wife, which is at Exh 354. He has stated that he had given the details of this Lease Agreement to CBI and that the CBI did not accept the same and instead told him to produce the same in the Court as they had not seen the said couple. He has deposed that Ashok Rishi is currently settled in USA and that he had given the telephonic details to PI RA Yadav under letter dated 16.9.2000, which was sent by registered post. He has produced the copy of the said letter along with AD card which are at Exh 355 collectively.

It may be mentioned here that the Investigating Officer Shri Mukherjee has stated in his cross-examination that his investigation revealed that the accused had a flat in New Delhi. He has stated that he does not remember whether the accused had a flat in New Delhi. He has stated that he does not remember whether the accused had continued to be the owner of the said flat in New Delhi while he was posted in Goa. He has stated that his investigation did not reveal that any other person other than the family of the accused was residing in the said flat in New Delhi. He has further stated that he does not recollect whether the accused had informed him that he had leased the said flat. He has denied the suggestion that he is well aware that the accused has leased the flat in New Delhi. He has further stated that he does not recollect whether the accused had given to him the copy of the Lease Deed dated 3.11.1993 executed between him and one Ashok Rishi. When he was specifically asked whether he had interrogated Ashok Rishi, he stated that Ashok Rishi was not available at the given address. He has further stated that he does not recollect the address of Ashok Rishi. He has stated that he cannot say anything to the suggestion that the accused had earned over ₹2,50,000 during the check period from the rent received by leasing flat.

It may be mentioned here that the prosecution has not denied that the accused is the owner of the flat. The lease agreement at Exh 353 clearly indicates that the accused had informed the Investigating Officer about the execution of the Lease Agreement. However, a perusal of the letter at Exh 355 clearly indicates that the accused had informed the Investigating Officer about the execution of the Lease Agreement, the rent received and deposited in his account in Canara Bank, New Delhi. He had also furnished the address as well as the telephonic contact of Ashok Rishi. The Investigating Officer had not taken any pains to contact the said Ashok Rishi and verify the bank statement number 4 of the accused as regards the execution of the Lease Agreement and receipt of the rent from Ashok Rishi. Investigating Officer has also not verified the Bank account of the accused or the entries made in the passbook in order to ascertain the veracity of the statement of the accused regarding the receipt of the rent from the said Ashok Rishi and his wife. The prosecution has not given any reason for presuming that the initial lease was fraudulent. Besides, the lease cannot be termed fraudulent merely ecause the lessees has continued to be in possession of the flat without renewing the lease agreement in writing. Under the circumstances, there is no reason to disbelieve the case of the accused that he had leased the flat at Alaknanda, New Delhi to Ashok Rishi and his wife and that he had derived the rent of ₹2,49,316 during the check period. Hence, in my considered view, the said amount of ₹2,49,316 needs to be added to the income of the accused during the check period.

Income from Sale of Boxer Pups

Learned Advocate Shri JP D'Souza has argued that the prosecution has not considered the fact that the accused had earned an income of ₹1,64,000 from breeding and selling Boxer pups. Learned PP Shri Vaz has argued that the accused had not produced any document to show that he had received such amount and that the claim of the accused is incorrect.

In this regard, the accused has deposed that his wife used to breed and sell Boxer pups from 1991 till 1998 during his stay in New Delhi and in Goa. He has stated that Dr Mrs Kharab was the Vet in New Delhi whereas Dr G Pinto is the Vet in Goa. He has deposed that they used to get about one or two litters of pups every year with 4 to 5 pups a litter. He has deposed that the pups were sold at the rate of ₹4,000 to ₹5,000 per pup. He has deposed that they had earned an amount of ₹1,64,000 during the seven year period and that these details were provided to the CBI Officers along with the Vets and are reflected in the statement number 4 at Exh 109 despite which the CBI Officer has not included the same in his income. A perusal of the entry at serial number 14 of statement number 4 (Exh 109) also shows that the accused had disclosed the names and addresses of the Vets attending to the pups. The accused has also produced Canine Vaccination Certificate at Exh 417.

The accused had also examined Veterinary Surgeon Dw2 Dr Gustav Pinto. He has deposed that he is working in Government Veterinary Department Animal Husbandry since the year 1987. He has stated that in the year 1995 he was posted at Panaji. He has produced the daily *Gomantak Times* dated 18.12.1994 wherein it was reported that the accused was the winner of the best Goan Boxer dogs. He has deposed that the Boxer dog belonging to the accused had also won the prize as best of breed at the dog show organized on 11.12.1994 at the Jawaharlal Nehru Stadium at Fatorda. He has deposed that whenever a dog was brought for a vaccination, he used to affix vaccination sticker on a booklet and that he also affixed his stamp and signature on the said booklet. He has deposed that on an average a Boxer female reproduces about 5 to 6 pups per litter and a Boxer female adult would litter once or twice a year. He has deposed that the cost of Boxer pup in the year 1995 was approximately about ₹5,000. He has deposed that the accused used to bring his dogs to the Government Veterinary Hospital for treatment and vaccination. He has deposed that the accused used to breed pups for sale. In his cross-examination, he has stated that the accused had a pair of male and female Boxer dog.

Dw7 Promila Menon, the wife of the accused, has also deposed that she and her husband used to breed Boxer pups from 1987 onwards. She has deposed that the dogs were treated by the Vet Surgeons Dr Mrs Kharab in New Delhi and Dr Mr Gustav Pinto in Goa. She has deposed that their dogs had participated in dog shows in Delhi as well as in Goa and that they had won prizes in the form of silver medals. She has stated that they used to sell one Boxer pup for ₹4,000 to ₹5,000 and that during the check period from 1991 to 1998 they had earned approximately about ₹1,64,000 from the sale of Boxer pups. She has stated that the said amount is also reflected in the statement at Exh 109. Though the accused had given the details of the dogs including the names of the Vets, the prosecution has chosen not to record the statements of the Veterinary Surgeon in order to ascertain the veracity of the statement of accused.

It is also pertinent to note that the prosecution witness Pw46 Mohammad Ali has admitted that the accused was in the business of breeding and selling pups. He has stated that in the year 1989-1990 he had purchased two pups from the accused for ₹ 10,000. He has also deposed that the accused was doing the business of breeding and selling pups even subsequently.

The aforesaid evidence clearly supports the contention of the accused that he was breeding Boxer pups. The evidence of the Veterinary Dr Gustav Pinto clearly indicates that on an average an adult Boxer female litters once or twice in a year and reproduces about 5 to 6 pups per litter. The evidence of this witness indicates that the cost of a Boxer pup in the year of 1995 was approximately about ₹ 5,000. Even if it is considered that the Boxer female had littered only once in a year and produced 5 pups on an average, the annual income from the sale of 5 pups at the rate of ₹ 5,000 each, the income works out to ₹ 25,000 per annum and it comes to ₹ 2,00,000 for eight years. Considering this fact, there is no reason to disbelieve the statement of the accused that he had earned ₹ 1,64,000 through the sale of Boxer pups. Hence, an amount of ₹ 1,64,000 is required to be credited to the income of the accused.

Credit Shares Deposited in Syndicate Bank

The accused has deposed that the prosecution has not considered an amount of ₹ 1,19,468, being credit of shares deposited in his account in Syndicate Bank. The said credits are reflected in Exh 58 being the ledger of

Syndicate Bank. The said credits are reflected in Exh 58 being the ledger of Syndicate Bank, account number 17958, which is in the name of the accused and the said entries are made between January 1994 to March 1994. The accused has deposed that the total amount of ₹1,19,468 being credit of shares was credited in his account in the month of January 1994 till March 1994 and that the said entries are reflected in Exh 58 produced through Pw4 Krishna. The accused has deposed that he had infoımed the CBI about the said credit vide letter dated 28.9.1999 along with enclosures. It is to be noted that Dw1 was not at all cross-examined and that there is no reason to believe the said statement. Hence in my considered view an income of ₹1,19,468 is to be considered as the income of the accused.

Interest on FDRs

The accused has stated that an amount of ₹83,812 is also not considered. It is not in dispute that the FDRs created in 1995 for total sum of ₹2,75,000 were reinvested/renewed with SBI in 2017 with maturity amount aggregating to ₹35,881. Though the prosecution has stated that an amount of ₹2,75,000 is an asset, the interest of ₹83,812 has not been shown as the income. In my considered view, the said interest of ₹83,812 is to be considered as income even though the same was not released to the accused.

Previous Earnings

The accused has deposed that an amount of ₹5,46,237.60 being his earning prior to the check period has not been considered. Dw1 has deposed that he was employed in the Indian Navy from October 1965 till November 1994 and thereafter he took over the assignment as Chairman and Managing Director of Goa Shipyard Ltd. The accused has deposed that he was on deputation in the Indian High Commission London between October 1980 to July 1983. He has produced a letter issued by Naval Pay Office, Mumbai, at Exh 348 collectively indicating that his net earning from March 1966 to December 1990 was ₹4,36,305.76. He has stated that the salary drawn by him during the period he was on deputation is not included in the statement. He has deposed that during the deputation period of 32 months, he had received total amount of ₹2,46,492. He has produced a letter dated 19.6.2009 at Exh 418 collectively which shows the details of the pay and allowances received by the accused during his deputation as Deputy Naval Advisor in the Indian High Commission at London. He has deposed that the said amount earned by him during his employment abroad has not been included by the CBI. It is argued on behalf of the prosecution that the income prior to the check period is not to be considered for computation of DA and further that the said amount is in the form of reimbursement. It is to be noted that the prosecution has not specifically denied that the accused had received this amount, but had merely claimed that the accused had not informed the CBI about the same. The contention of the prosecution that the earnings prior to the check period cannot be considered as the income also cannot be accepted. In the case of Krishnanand *vs* State of MP (CDJ 1976 SC 293), it has been held that some part of savings was considered view, 20% of the previous income which works out to ₹ 1,09,247 can be considered as savings and the same can be credited to the income during the check period.

Allowance on Foreign Tours

Learned Advocate Shri JP D'Souza has argued that the prosecution has not considered the fact that during his trips to foreign countries, the accused was entitled to foreign exchange in addition to his regular salary and that he was paid allowance of US $ 500 per day. Learned PP Shri Vaz has argued that the foreign allowance are in fact reimbursement of the expenditure incurred on foreign tours and same cannot be considered as part of his income.

The accused has also stated that during his tours to foreign countries between December 1994 to May 1998, in addition to his salary he was paid foreign allowance of US $ 500 per day. He has deposed that during his tenure of five years, he had visited eleven countries and was paid total foreign allowance equivalent to the tune of ₹21,73,797. The accused has deposed that the amount received was paid in advance to meet expenses towards hotel, travelling, food, etc and that he was not required to refund the balance. He has deposed that since he was received by Host Department and Companies, he was only spending on hotel accommodation. The other expenses towards travelling, food, etc, were taken care of by Host Department and Company and that on an average he used to save a minimum of $250 per day. He has stated that on the said basis, he had saved an amount equivalent to ₹4,34,759 which on an average is 20% of the foreign exchange given to him. The accused has stated that the said amount is not included in his income.

In this regard Pw1 S Ananthasayanam, General Manager (Finance), Goa Shipyard, has stated in his cross-examination that the accused was entitled to foreign exchange whenever he was sent to foreign countries. He has stated that for the period between December 1994 to May 1998 the accused was sent on foreign tours on total eleven occasions. He has produced the statement at Exh 32 which shows the details of the foreign tours made by the accused between December 1994 to May 1998 and the amount paid to the accused in foreign currency as well the equivalent value of the same in Indian rupees. He has stated that the said amount was in addition to the salary received by the accused. He has further stated that some people try to save foreign exchange and even if it is saved, the amount is not returned to the company. He has stated that there is no rule prescribed for the return of the same.

The evidence on record clearly indicates that the accused had received an amount equivalent to ₹21,73,797 towards foreign allowance. The evidence of the accused further indicates that he had to spend only on his hotel accommodation and the other expenses were paid by the Host Companies. Considering this aspect, in my considered view, 20% of allowance which works out to ₹4,34,759.40 can be considered as savings and are required to be included in the income of the accused.

TA/DA on Official Journey in India

The accused has stated that the prosecution has not considered an amount of ₹76,466 which was paid towards TA/DA while he was on temporary duty. The accused has deposed that while he was on the official journey in India he was paid ₹250 per day towards hotel, travelling and food expenses. The accused has stated that he had received total amount of ₹76,466 which is reflected in the statement at Exh 33. The Investigating Officer has admitted that he has not included the same amount in the income of the accused as the same is reimbursement of daily expenses.

It is to be noted that the evidence of the accused clearly indicates that all the expenses towards hotel, travelling, food, etc, were actually borne by GSL. Thus being the case, 25% of the said amount which works out to ₹ 1,19,116 is considered as savings and the said amount of ₹ 1,19,116 is credited in the income of the accused.

The accused has therefore proved by preponderance of probabilities that an income of ₹ 16,42,233.40 has not been considered by the prosecution. When the said income is added to the proved income, the total income of the accused during the check period works out to ₹ 80,51,319.58.

15

Expenditure-Related Issues

Quoting from the Judgement

Payment Made to Maria Park, Ernakulam

The prosecution has claimed that the accused has paid ₹55,010.30 to Maria Park, Ernakulam. Learned Advocate Shri JP D'Souza has argued that the said amount was paid by the mother and sister of the accused being the part of the wedding expense of the granddaughter/niece and that this fact was brought to the notice of the CBI Officer despite which the CBI Officer has not investigated into the matter. Learned PP Shri J Vaz has argued that the claim of the accused is not acceptable as the accused has not produced the relevant documents.

The prosecution has examined Pw3 Shri MV Das, the Managing Trustee of the Hotel Maria Park. This witness has deposed that Maria Park had issued a receipt dated 5.2.1998 to the accused for having received sum of ₹50,010 by cheque dated 5.2.1998 towards various expenses. He has produced the said receipt dated 5.2.1998 at Exh 163. A perusal of the said receipt indicates that the hotel had received from the accused a sum of ₹50,010.30 by cheque number SB/91/AA221884 and BA 639859 dated 5.2.1998 towards marriage expenses. It may be mentioned that in his cross-examination Pw33 was unable to state whether the cheque number 221884 was drawn on Bank of Baroda and whether it was issued by Mrs Leela B Menon from account number 7937. He was also unable to state whether the second cheque number 639859 was drawn on Federal Bank from account number 5437 for ₹25,010 of Anila Joseph.

It may be mentioned here that the accused has stated in this evidence that his daughter Nayana was married in January 1998 and that her marriage was solemnized in Cochin, Kerala. He has deposed that the wedding reception was held at Maria Park, Cochin. He has deposed that the major expenses towards the marriage were borne by him. However, being the first granddaughter, his mother and sister shared some of expenses. He has deposed that his sister Anila contributed ₹25,000 towards the marriage by issuing a cheque from Federal Bank, Edappally. He has produced a letter/certificate issued by Federal Bank at Exh 351 collectively certifying that an amount of

₹25,010.30 was paid to M/s Maria Park by cheque issued from the account of 5437 in the name of Mr MC Joseph and B Anila Joseph on 19.2.1998. The accused has also produced the copy of the passbook clearly indicates that an amount of ₹25,010 was debited from the said account on 19.2.1998 and was paid to Maria Park.

The accused has deposed that his mother Leela had paid ₹25,000 by cheque from her account in Bank of Baroda and that the said amount was paid to M/s Maria Park. The accused has produced the copy of the passbook at Exh 352. The said passbook pertains to account number 7937 of Bank of Baroda in the name of Leela Balakrishnan Menon and shows that an amount of ₹25,000 was debited from her account on 7.2.1998.

It may be mentioned here that the Investigating Officer Pw51 Shri Mukherjee has admitted in his cross-examination that an amount of ₹50,010 was paid to Maria Park by two cheques. Hence investigating agency was required to investigate whether this amount was paid by the accused or on behalf of the accused. It may be mentioned that Pw51 Shri Mukherjee has admitted that he had not investigated to find out whether the said cheques were drawn from any particular account as according to him at the relevant time, the investigation of the said two cheques was being conducted by other two officers. He has stated that he did not direct subordinate officers to find out from whose account the said cheques were issued as according to him he did not find it necessary. He has admitted that the number of the said two cheques were reflected in the letter/certificate (Exh 163) issued by Maria Park. He was unable to deny the suggestion that the said two cheques were not from the account of the accused and that they were in fact issued from the account of the mother and sister of accused. He has volunteered to say that he had conducted investigation to know the source of income or financial condition of the mother of the accused and that he found that the mother of accused was dependent solely on the accused. This witness has stated that he did not verify the Bank account of the mother of accused. He did not investigate to find out the bank balance of the mother of the accused from starting point of the cheque period. He has stated that he did not investigate to find out how much gold she had at the time of the cheque period. He claims that he had conducted search of the house of the mother of the accused and that he did not find any gold, or cash or other valuables. He admits that there is no *panchanama* of the search of the house of accused. He has admitted that he has not produced any material on record to show the financial status of the mother of the accused had issued the cheque in favour of Maria Park to contribute towards the wedding of her granddaughter.

The evidence on record clearly indicates that the said two cheques for ₹55,010 were not issued by the accused from his account but were issued by his mother and sister. The Investigating Officer had not checked the bank accounts of the mother of the accused and has not produced any material on record to indicate that the mother of the accused and was not in sound financial condition or that she was totally dependant on accused. In the absence of any house search *panchanama* or other material on record I find it difficult to believe that the Investigating Officer had all the details of the cheque and was in a position to investigate the same. The Investigating Officer has not only failed to investigate the same but has boldly claimed that it was not necessary to do so. In my considered view, without such investigation, the Investigating Officer could not have attributed the said amount to the accused. Hence the prosecution has failed to establish that the accused had paid an amount of ₹55,010 to Maria Park. Consequently, the said amount needs to be deducted from the expense list.

Furnitures Purchased (as Declared in Property Return in Form 1-4)

The case of the prosecution is that the accused had incurred expenses of ₹63,300 towards purchase of furniture. In this regard, the prosecution has examined Under-Secretary (Vigilance) Pw19 AP Khathria. He has deposed that as per the rules in force every government servant is required to file the property statement of the property acquired and disposed of every year. He has stated that by letter dated 14.9.1999 he had submitted to the CBI the statement of the properties purchased and disposed by the accused. The said letter and six statements are at Exh 109. He has stated that the statement number 3 pertains to the movable properties for the period ending 31st December, 1998. He has stated that as per the said statement the accused had purchased carpets, radio, TV, VCR, tape-recorder, etc he has stated that value of TV is shown as ₹ 12,000, the value of VCR is shown as ₹ 1,000, the value of refrigerator is shown as ₹ 8,000, the value of camera is shown as ₹ 1,500, wall paintings as ₹ 3,000, Indian crockery as ₹ 5,000, imported crockery as 120 pounds, a mixer 50 pounds and cut glasses worth ₹ 25,000. In his cross-examination he has stated that the carpets were purchased in the year 1988, the mixer was purchased between 1982-92, the crockery was purchased in the year 1980-81. He has further stated that the glassware was with the accused for about 35 years and it was purchased from the beginning of his Navy days in the year 1969. The evidence of the aforesaid witness does not indicate that the accused had purchased the said items during the check period. This being the case, the said amount needs to be deducted from the list of expenses.

Expenditure Incurred on Education of Dependant Daughter at AB Shetty Dental College, Mangalore

The case of prosecution is that the accused had incurred expenditure of ₹4,01,521 on education of his daughter at AB Shetty Dental College, Mangalore. Learned Advocate Shri JP D'Souza has argued that the accused was married in the year 1998 and that the sum of ₹54,450 was paid by her husband. He has further argued that the letter at Exh 137 is not proved the expenses of ₹40,000 towards rent and ₹56,771 towards mess deposit. Learned PP Shri J Vaz has argued that the evidence of Pw25 amply that the accused had incurred expenditure of ₹4,01,520 towards educational expenses of his daughter.

It may be mentioned that the prosecution has examined the Superintendent of Shetty Dental College Pw25 Shri Prabhakar. He has produced a letter at Exh 136 whereby the details of the amount received from Nayana Menon for her BDS and MDS courses in AB Shetty Dental College at Mangalore are given. He has also produced a letter at Exh 137 issued by the Principal Shri M Shetty wherein the details of the payment including the payment made towards hostel rent and mess deposit are shown. This witness has identified the signature of the Principal and has confirmed the contents of the said letter and as such there is no reason to discard or disbelieve the contents of the said letter. In his cross-examination

Pw25 Shri Prabhakar has stated that the said amount paid by the student herself. He was unable to say anything to the suggestion that a sum of ₹54,450 was paid by the husband of the student Nayana Menon. He has also stated that it is possible that an amount of ₹10,127 was paid from the bank account of the said student. He has stated that the amount of ₹4,500 which is shown as caution deposit has been refunded.

It may be mentioned here that Dw1 has deposed that his daughter was studying in AB Shetty Dental College at Mangalore from 1991 to 1998. He has deposed that his daughter was married in January 1990 and that ₹54,450 being the fees of the final year and which is reflected in the statement at Exh 136 were paid by her husband Shri Subash Raj on 16.5.1998. He has stated that the said amount is wrongly shown as his expense. The evidence on record clearly indicates that Nayana Menon was married in January 1998. The prosecution has not investigated whether the amount of ₹54,450 being the fees of the final year were paid by the accused or by the husband of the said Nayana Menon. In the absence of such cogent evidence the amount of ₹54,450 needs to be deducted from the expense list. Thus, the evidence on record shows that the accused had incurred expenditure of ₹3,42,571 towards educational expenses of his daughter Nayana Menon.

Payment Made to M/s Mubeen Air Travels, Vasco

It is the case of prosecution that the accused had paid ₹80,634 to M/s Mubeen Air Travels. Learned PP Shri Vaz has argued that the evidence of Pw23 clearly shows that the accused had paid the said amount in his personal capacity. Learned PP Shri Vaz has argued that the prosecution has proved that the accused had incurred the said expenses. Learned Advocate Shri JP D'Souza has argued that Pw23 has not identified the accused as the same person whose name is recorded in the register. He has further argued that the details of the payment are not recorded in the register. It is further argued that the evidences were borne by the accused or his family members and that the Investigating Officer has not made any attempt to counter check the audited statement of GSL as regards these expenses.

The prosecution has examined Pw25 Prakash Vasudev who is an accountant with Mubeen Air Travels. The witness has deposed that the accused used to book air tickets in his individual as well as in official capacity. He has given the details of several air tickets booked in the name of Mrs G Menon, N Menon and BR Menon. He has stated that total amount of ₹80,634 was paid in respect of the said tickets. In his cross-examination he has stated that most of the amount covering ₹80,634 was paid by cheque. However, the details of the cheque are not mentioned in the register. He has stated that the cheque details are not mentioned in the register. He has stated that the cheque details and the destination are not mentioned in the register. He had stated that the register does not mention the address of G Menon and N Menon. He has stated that the register also does not disclose whether N Menon was married or not. He was unable to state whether the air fare of Mrs N Menon was paid by her husband and whether Mrs G Menon had paid the air fare in respect of tickets booked in her name. He has further stated in his cross-examination that he is unable to state whether the names figuring in the register are in respect of persons who purchased the tickets or are of the passengers. He has stated that he had never seen Admiral BR Menon VSM or his family members. He has also stated that he does not know Mrs G Menon in whose names the tickets were booked. In the absence of clear evidence to show that these tickets were booked by the accused either in his name or in the name of his family members, the expenses in respect of these tickets cannot be attributed to the personal expenses of the accused and hence an amount of ₹80,634 needs to be deducted from the expenses.

Payment Made to M/s Gateway Travels, Vasco (M/s Menezes Air Travel)

The case of prosecution is that the accused had paid ₹1,22,145 to M/s Gateway Travels, Vasco. The prosecution had examined Pw41 Sanjay Shety, who was the sub-agent of Gateway Travels. The evidence of this witness cannot be looked into as his examination in chief was not completed and he was not subjected to cross-examination. This being the case, an amount of ₹1,22,145 allegedly paid to M/s Gateway Travels needs to be deducted from the expenses.

Payment Made to Architect for Preparation of Plan for House at Cochin

The case of prosecution is that the accused had paid ₹55,000 to the Architect for preparation of plan of his house. Learned Advocate Shri JP D'Souza has argued that the said amount was paid after the check period and cannot be considered whereas Learned PP Shri Vaz has argued that it is highly improbable and beyond imagination that professional would receive his fees two years after completion of work.

The prosecution has examined the Architect Pw34 Ramesh Tharakan. He has deposed in the month of January 1999 the accused had approached him to redesign his house and that he had charged ₹50,000 towards his professional fees. In his cross-examination he has stated that the said fees were paid to him in the year 2000. The said statement clearly indicates that the Architect's fees of ₹50,000 were paid after the check period. This witness was neither re-examined by the prosecution and as such, there are no reasons to disbelieve the statement made by him. His evidence clearly show that he had received his fees of ₹50,000 after the check period and hence the same needs to be deducted from the expenses.

Cost of 02 Economy Class Air Tickets for Bombay-Heathrow-Toronto-Paris-Geneva-New York-Bombay

The case of prosecution was that the accused had paid ₹1,88,710 towards cost of two economic class air tickets from Bombay-Heathrow-Toronto-Paris-Geneva-New York-Bombay.

Learned PP Shri Vaz has argued that the evidence of Pw24 Shri Pawan Kumar vis-a-vis the certificate at Exh 134 amply proves that the accused had incurred the said expenditure on his travel whereas Learned Advocate Shri JP D'Souza has argued that the accused had travelled abroad in the year 1994 and all the details are available in Passport. He has deposed that the payment of ₹1,10,000 was made by the accused by cheque drawn on Grindlays Bank. He therefore claims that an amount of ₹78,710 has to be credited to the accused.

It may be mentioned that the prosecution has examined Pw24 Pawan Kumar who was working as Customer Relations Manager with Air India in New Delhi. He had issued the certificate dated 16.8.1999 at Exh 134 certifying that the economy class fare for travel on Air India on the route Bombay-Toronto-Geneva-

London-Toronto-New York-Paris-Bombay, during the month of August, 1994. He also stated that he does not know whether the same rate was applicable to the flight from Bombay-Geneva-London-New York and return. He was unable to state whether the fare for the said route was ₹55,000. He was also unable to state whether two tickets were purchased for the said route for ₹1,10,000. It may be mentioned here that accused has deposed that he and his wife had made overseas trips in the year 1994 in order to attend the graduation of his daughter in USA. He has stated that during the relevant period he was posted at Mumbai as Rear Admiral. He has deposed that he had travelled on 7.5.1994 to Geneva and on 13.5.1994 to London and on 17.5.1994 from London to New York and that he returned to Mumbai on 12.6.1994 by direct flight of Air India. He has stated that during his stay in USA he had travelled to Canada and back by road. He has stated that all the details of his overseas trips are available in the passport and Visa record. He has deposed that he had purchased the tickets for USA from Concord Travels Mumbai and paid ₹1,10,000 by cheque drawn on ANZ Grindlays Bank. He has deposed that the said information was given to the investigating agency vide letter dated 28.9.1999. The Investigating Officer has not denied having received such information but has claimed that he does not remember whether such information was given by the accused.

It may be mentioned that the accused has produced the copy of the statement of the bank showing relevant entry dated 8.7.1994. He has further deposed that he had not travelled to Paris or Toronto on the stated dates. He has further stated that he had written to ANZ Grindlays Bank asking for the payment made by him by cheque. He has stated that he had received the reply from the said bank, now Standard Chartered Bank stating that they are unable to trace the details since the transaction is more than eight years old. The aforesaid evidence clearly indicates that the accused had not incurred an expenses of ₹ 1,88,710 but had incurred an amount of ₹ 1,10,000 which paid by the cheque number 331359 dated 7.7.1994 from Agency was required to investigate this aspect since the said information was already furnished by the accused. However, the investigating agency has failed to investigate the said aspect. Consequently, I am inclined to hold that the expenses incurred by the accused on his foreign tours were ₹ 1,10,000 needs to be deducted from the expense list.

16

Assets-Related Issues

In the case of assets I am only bringing one or two examples where the CBI has gone out of their way to prove the inflated value of my assets or add others' assets as that of mine.

Quoting from the Judgement

Plot Numbers 14, 18, 38 and 39, Cortalim, Kesarwal, Goa

The case of the prosecution is that the accused had purchased four plots being plot numbers 14, 18, 38 and 39 at Cortalim, Kesarwal, Goa for a total price of ₹9,38,062. Learned PP Shri Vaz has argued that the evidence of Pw29 Sumita Walavalkar, Pw30 Mukta Ganesh Daivarjna vis-a-vis the documents at Exh 154 to 156 amply prove that the accused had purchased the said four plots at Cortalim. Learned Advocate Shri

JP D'Souza has argued that the evidence adduced by the prosecution amply proves that the said plots were purchased by the accused on behalf of Commander PS Sachedev. He has argued that the accused had submitted the details of the sale transaction to the Vigilance Department and that the accused had also given all the details of the said transaction, including the bank accounts to the CBI Officer. He has argued that the Investigating Officer has not considered the documents and has also not investigated whether the money was paid by the accused or by Sachedev. On the contrary, the evidence adduced by the accused amply proves that the said purchase was in the nature of *Benami* construction on behalf of Commander Sachedev and as such the entire amount in respect of the said four plots needs to be deducted from the said holdings of the accused.

In this regard, the prosecution has examined Pw29 Smt Sumita T Walavalkar. This witness has deposed that she owned a plot of land at Mohiddin Estates on Airport Road at Vasco and that she was interested in selling the same. She has deposed that she knew the accused and that sometimes in the year 1996 he had told her that he was interested in buying the said plot. She has deposed that she has sold the plot to the accused for ₹2,89,000 and that the accused has purchased the said plot in the name of his daughter Nidhiya Menon. She has stated that the accused had initially paid an amount ₹10,000 in cash and the balance amount ₹2,79,600 was paid by the accused in cheque drawn on Canara Bank, Delhi Branch. She has produced the sale deed 26.12.1996 at Exh 154. In her cross-examination she has stated that she does not have any receipt in respect of ₹10,000 received by her.

The prosecution has also examined Pw30 Mukta Ganesh Daivarjna. She has deposed that she was a partner of Kesarwal Real Estate. She has further deposed that the accused had approached the firm for buying the three plots number 18, 38, 39 and that the said plots were sold to Nayana Menon and Mrs Promila Menon. She has stated that to Nayana Menon she sold the plot vide Deed dated 28.5.1997 for ₹2,50,000. She has further deposed that the stamp duty of ₹17,320 and the registration fee of ₹2,330 was paid by the accused. She has deposed that the other two plots were sold to Promila Menon for ₹2,16,500 and ₹1,10,750. She has deposed that the accused had paid ₹19,500 towards stamp duty and ₹2,330 towards registration fees. She has produced the three sale deeds which are at Exh 156 collectively. In her cross-examination she has stated that the amount was paid by two Demand Drafts bearing numbers 205107 and 105108 for ₹3,10,250. She has stated that there were two other DDs bearing number 705110 and DD number 605111 for ₹1,25,000 each. She has stated that she does not know from whose account the said Demand Drafts were drawn. She has stated that she had not accompanied the accused to purchase the stamp papers. She has further stated that she does not know who had purchased the said stamp paper.

The evidence of both these witnesses indicates that the accused had purchase of said plots. The evidence on record further indicates that Pw29 had executed sale deed at Exh 154 in favour of Nidhiya Menon whereby she had sold plot number 14 for ₹2,89,000 whereas Pw30 had executed three sale deeds at Exh 156 collectively in favour of Nayana Menon and Promila Menon.

The case of accused is that the said four plots were purchased by his wife and two daughters for the purpose of constructing a housing colony as proposed by his friend Commander Sachedev from Delhi and the entire money for the said project was spent by said Sachedev. In the case of M Krishna Reddy *vs* State Deputy Superintendent of Police, Hyderabad (CDJ 1991 SC 200), the Apex Court has reiterated the principles laid down in case of Krishnanand Agnihotri *vs* State MP (AIR 1977 SC 796) wherein it was held that "it is well-settled that the burden of showing that a particular transaction is *Benami* and the owner is not real owner always rests on the person asserting it to be so and this burden has to be strictly discharged by addicting legal evidence of definite character which would either directly prove the fact of *Benami* or establish circumstances unerringly and reasonably raising an inference of that fact. The essence of *Benami* is the intention of the parties and not unoften, such intention is shrouded in a thick veil which cannot be easily pierced through. But such difficulties do not relieve the person asserting the transaction to be *Benami* or the serious onus that rests on him not justify the acceptance of mere conjectures of surmises as a substitute of proof."

In the present case, the accused has deposed that the said plots were purchased for constructing a housing colony as proposed by his friend late Commander Sachedev from Delhi. He has deposed that the entire money for said project was paid by Sachedev through three Demand Drafts and one cheque in the name of the sellers. He has produced letter at Exh 356. He has stated that the total consideration for the said plots was ₹8,39,885 which was paid by three Demand Drafts of ₹1,25,000 each and the fourth Demand Draft for ₹1,85,250 besides a cheque for ₹2,79,600. He has deposed that the stamp duty and the registration charges amounting to ₹79,076 were also borne by said Sachedev. He has deposed that the sale transaction in respect of four plots and funding by Commander Sachedev was disclosed by him in his statements of immovable property submitted to Vigilance Department of Goa Shipyard as per the rules. The photocopies of the extracts of statements are at Exh 357. He has further deposed that vide letter dated 28.8.1999 he had forwarded to the Director of CBI statement of entire income and expenditure including the disclosure relating to the said four plots and that the copy of the same was marked to Central Vigilance Commission and also to the Investigating Officer. He has deposed that on account of the demise of his friend Commander Sachedev, the entire scheme of having a Naval Colony fell through and as such, by three sale deeds they parted possession of the said plots in favour of Gundeep Sachedev. He has produced the said three sale deeds all dated 7.8.1999 which are at Exh 358 collectively. He has deposed that no consideration passed hands and that the record of the same is made in each of these sale deeds and that Gundeep Sachedev has acknowledged the same. He has deposed that the stamp duty in respect of the three sale deeds has been borne by Gundeep Sachedev. He has denied the suggestion that he has given unaccounted money to Sachedev and that Sachedev had issued Demand Drafts and the cheques at his instance.

It is to be noted that the evidence of the Senior Manager of Canara Bank, New Delhi, Pw26 Uppoor Ranganath Adiga and Senior Manager in Canara Overseas Branch, New Delhi, Pw27 VK Goel proves that said Sachedev was Director of M/s Makalu

Consulting Engineering Pvt Ltd and that he had his account in the said banks. They have identified his specimen signatures on Exhs 146 collectively and Exh 148. In his cross-examination, Pw27 has deposed that the current account 1343 of Canara Bank, Hauz Khas, New Delhi, was in the name of M/s Instant Autogas Manufacturing Pvt Ltd and that the account holder was Commander P Sachedev and his family. He has deposed that the Demand Drafts number 605111 dated 6.5.1996 for ₹1,25,000, Demand Draft number 105108 dated 6.5.1996 for ₹1,25,000, Demand Draft number 205107 dated 6.5.1996 for ₹1,85,250 and Demand Draft number 705110 dated 6.5.1996 for ₹1,25,000, all favouring Kesarwal Real Estate were issued from the account of M/s Instant Autogas Equipment. He has also stated that the cheque number 210227 dated 16.11.1996 for ₹2,79,600 was debited to the account number GA1174 of M/s Makalu Consulting Engineering Pvt Ltd on 27.11.1996. He has stated that the said account is in the name of Commander Sachedev and his family members/heirs. This witness was re-examined by the prosecution wherein he has stated that he was not in a position to state as to who had made the deposit in the accounts of M/s Makalu Consulting Engineering from which account the four Demand Drafts were issued in favour of Kesarwal Estate. However, interestingly it was not suggested to this witness that the accused had deposited the money in any of the accounts of Commander Sachedev.

The accused has also examined Dw3 Gundeep Sachedev. He has deposed that he knows the accused since his childhood. Dw3 has deposed that his father and the accused were friends and that they were working together for Indian Navy. Dw3 has further deposed that the accused purchased four plots at Kesarwal on their behalf and that the payment in respect of the three plots was made by Demand Drafts in the name of M/s Instant Autogas Equipment Pvt Ltd and the fourth payment was made by cheque to M/s Makalu Consulting Engineering Pvt Ltd he has stated that the total amount paid was ₹8.5 lakh. He has stated that both the above companies were founded by his father and had their accounts in Canara Bank, Hauz Khas, New Delhi. He has deposed that the same was paid in cash between 1996 to 1997. He has stated that the said four plots were purchased with an intention of starting a Friendship Naval Colony. This witness has further deposed that since the project did not materialise, in the year 1999 he got the said plots transferred in his name vide sale deeds at Exh 358 collectively and took possession of the same. He has identified his signature on the sale deeds at Exh 358 collectively. In his cross-examination he has stated that he is the Director of M/s Instant Autogas Equipments Pvt Ltd and M/s Makalu Consulting

Engineering Pvt Ltd since about 1997. This statement is not challenged.

It is to be noted that the prosecution has not disputed that the Demand Drafts issued by Sachedev. Though it was suggested that the accused had given money to Sachedev, the investigating agency had made absolutely no efforts to find out whether the accused had laundered the money or that the accused had advanced the money to said Sachedev for issuing the said Demand Drafts and the cheque.

The evidence of Dw1 clearly indicates that he had disclosed the said transactions in the statement of immovable property submitted to Vigilance Department of GSL as per the rules. It is also be noted that Pw19 AP Khathria has stated that he has given to the CBI the statement regarding purchase and disposal of the property by the accused. This witness has stated that the said statement showed that the investments in the Kesarwal Estates were made by Demand Drafts which were directly paid by Commander Sachedev.

It is also to be noted that Pw51 had produced the personal service file of accused which was said to contain personal records of accused. Pw53 Vajallu, the General Manager of GSL has admitted that the accused was filing his returns of assets and liabilities and that in the year 1999, Venu Gopal, who was then working as Chief Manager had handed over sealed envelope along with the personal records of the accused. He has deposed that he had gone through the personal file of the accused at Exh 245. He claims that there is no document in the file of the accused at Exh 245 to show that the accused had submitted returns of assets and liabilities. In his cross-examination this witness has stated that no action was taken against the accused for not filing the property returns. He has stated that one sealed envelope which was given to him by Venu Gopal, then Chief Vigilance Officer was containing he property return documents. He has stated that he had handed over the said sealed envelope to the CBI Officer during the course of investigation of the case. He has stated that the said sealed envelope was opened in his presence and it contained the documents pertaining to the property of the accused and that he does not recollect whether the said documents disclosed acquisition of four plots on long term loan from Sachedev. This witness also has stated that he does not remember whether the sealed envelope also contained the letter dated 2.4.1996 of Commander Sachedev addressed to the accused on the letterhead of M/s Instant Autogas Manufacturing Pvt Ltd wherein Commander Sachedev had proposed the purchase of the said four plots. This witness has also stated that he does not recollect whether the said letter was furnished by the accused along with the said property returns.

It is pertinent to note that Pw51 has admitted that the investigations revealed that the accused had produced before Pw53 RK Vajallu one sealed envelope containing assets statement. He has stated that he had not relied upon the said documents because the information pertaining to the said four plots was false. In his cross-examination, he has stated that he had read the contents of the said documents in presence of Pw53 RK Vajallu and that the said documents pertained to the property returns of the accused. He has stated that he does not have the said documents in his possession. He has further stated that he did not return the documents which were produced by Vajallu in a sealed envelope. He was also unable to say who is in possession of the said documents. He has denied the suggestion that he had suppressed the said documents as they were not supporting the prosecution case. He was unable to deny a specific suggestion that the said documents clearly indicates that the said four plots which were purchased by the accused in the name of his wife and daughters were actually financed by Commander Sachedev. He has further stated that item wise list was prepared in respect of the said documents found in the seizure list. He has stated that the seizure list was not filed along with the chargesheet as it was not required. He has stated that the documents found in the sealed envelope were shown to the accused for his explanation. He was unable to state when the said documents were shown to the accused. He has also stated that he had not re-sealed the envelope handed over by Pw53 and which was opened by him. It was suggested to him that he had financed the purchase of the said plots and that the said letters were signed by Shri Sachedev. To this suggestion, this witness has stated that the said letters were forged. It was also suggested to Pw51 that the said envelope also contained details of Demand Drafts indicating the purchase of the properties. To this suggestion the witness has once again replied that the letters of Sachedev were forged. He has stated that the letters found in the envelope and which were allegedly signed by Sachedev were forwarded for handwriting expert opinion. He has stated that he did not draw a *panchanama* while forwarding the said letters to the handwriting expert. When it was suggested to this witness that he had not sent the letter to handwriting expert, he stated that he did not remember. He has stated that the sale transaction at Exh 154 shows that the sale price was paid by cheque. He has stated that he did not investigate as to from whose account payment was made. He was specifically questioned as to why he did not make any enquiry with Canara Bank, Delhi regarding the accounts pertaining to the said cheque. This witness has stated that the very basis of the loan theory purportedly given by Shri Sachedev were forged. He has stated that he did not make any inquiry as to in whose name the account was standing in Canara Bank against whose name the cheque were issued. He has admitted that the said account might not have been in the name of accused or his family members. He has also admitted that the said cheques might not have been signed by the accused or his family members and that the same might have been signed by Commander Sachedev.

Pw51 has further deposed that he has also not investigated the mode of payment in respect of the other three plots purchased by sale deeds at Exh 156 collectively. He claims that such investigation was irrelevant as it was revealed that the documents were false. He has admitted that the Demand Drafts in respect of the three plots might not have been issued either by the accused or his family members. He has stated that he is not aware whether the Demand Drafts and cheques pertaining to the sale deeds at Exh 156 collectively were issued by Commander Sachedev.

The evidence on record indicates that the accused had furnished the details of the said plots in his statement/documents filed before the Vigilance Department of the Goa Shipyard. In my considered view, in the absence of any cogent material, the investigating agency could not have presumed that the documents were fabricated. Withholding these documents leads to an interference that prosecuting Agency was withholding material evidence which was not supporting the case of prosecution. The Prosecuting Agency has failed to investigate whether the amount paid to Kesarwal Estate by Demand Drafts was from the account of Commander Sachedev or whether the said amount was deposited by the accused in the account of Commander Sachedev. Under the circumferences, the defence raised by the accused is probable and hence, I am not inclined to consider the said four plots as the asset holdings of the accused.

Cost of Construction of House at Cochin

The case of the prosecution is that the accused had constructed a house at Cochin, the value of which is stated to be ₹ 19,69,965. Learned PP Shri J Vaz has argued that the evidence of Pw35 Shri TN Narayanan vis-a-vis the report at Exh 167 proves that the accused had incurred expenses of ₹ 19,69,965. He has further argued that the fact that Pw34 had received ₹ 50,000-55,000 as his commission also shows that the total cost of construction was between ₹ 30,00,000-35,00,000. He has argued that Pw35 had carried out the valuation in presence of the contractor Rajendra Kumar who could have furnished the correct information. He has argued that the architects usually estimates the cost on the lower side than the actual expenditure and as such, evidence of Pw35 cannot be discarded on the basis of the evidence of Pw34. Learned Advocate Shri JP D'Souza has argued that Pw35 had inspected the property after the check period. He has further argued that the evidence of the architect who was regularly visiting the site gives the correct stage and the valuation of the construction.

The prosecution has examined Assistant Engineer Pw35 Shri PN Narayan. He has deposed that at the request of CBI, he had valued that on 10.3.1999, he had valued two buildings of the accused. He has stated that the said buildings are situated in Kerala. He has stated that he inspected the said buildings in the presence of contractor Rajan, he carried put the measurements of the said two buildings and found that the said buildings were as per the building plan.

He has stated that after inspecting the building he prepared the report which is at Exh 167. He has stated that the total area of the main building was 580.11 square metres and that the total area of the outhouse was 88.55 square metres. He has stated that the total value of the main building comprising of the ground floor was ₹16,17,154 and that the value of the first floor was ₹81,500 and that the value of the outhouse was ₹2,18,309. He has stated that the valuation of the main building was done on the basis plinth area rates existing in the year 1982 and enhanced by the prevailing cost index of Cochin. He has stated that at the relevant time the cost of construction was ₹216 per square metre.

It may be mentioned that this witness had inspected the property after the check period and his cross-examination has revealed that he has no personal knowledge as to the stage of construction as on 31.12.1998. He was unable to state the extent of construction carried out between 1.1.1999 to 10.3.1999. He was unable to state anything to the suggestion that as on 31.12.1998 only the ground floor of the side building was constructed. He has admitted that as on the date of inspection. The ground floor had no doors, windows and that it was not plastered. He has stated that tiled were not fitted on the floor and that the electrical wiring was also not done. He has stated that the rates quoted by him were for the purpose of valuation and for the entire unit of construction which would be complete in all respects including plastering, doors, windows, electrical wirings, etc. He has stated that he has reduced the construction cost by 50% on the basis of own experience and assessment. He has denied the suggestion that only 23% of the construction was complete, he has stated that there is difference between Delhi rate and Kerala rate for construction. He has admitted that as on the date of the valuation no work was done above the lintel level on the first floor. He has considered extra 20% of the basic rate amounting to ₹91,100 for the sloppy portion. He has stated that he has considered the said extra rate of

20% on the basis of his experience. He has stated that there is no provision in the CPWD construction rules against construction for sloppy portion. He has denied the suggestion that his valuation is arbitrary. He was unable to state whether only the construction of the ground floor was completed as on 31.12.1998. He has admitted that door, windows, wiring, plastering and tiles were not fitted to the outhouse. He has denied the suggestion that at the time of valuation the actual value of the main building and the outhouse was around ₹ 11,00,000.

It is to be noted that the evidence of Architect Pw34 Ramesh Tharakan indicated that the total estimate of the house was ₹ 32,00,000. He has stated that the estimate of the completed work as on 31.12.98 was ₹ 11,34,968.34. He has stated that being an architect he used to supervise the construction and visit the same on weekly basis. He has stated that one Rajendra Kumar was engaged to do the field work and that he had given the name of the said Rajendra Kumar to the CBI. The prosecution for the reasons best known has not examined the said Rajendra Kumar.

It is also to be noted that the accused has deposed that the construction of the house was started in March 1998. He has stated that till December he had paid total sum ₹ 11,000 to Suburban Construction vide four cheques issued from his account in Syndicate

Bank and that he had brought the said fact to the notice of the investigating agency vide Exh 109 at the initial stage of inquiry. The said cheques which were issued in favour of Suburban Construction are indicated in Exh 58 which were produced through Pw4. There is no material on record to show that the investigating agency had interrogated any of the contractors of Suburban Construction and ascertained the veracity of the statement made by the accused.

It may be mentioned here that Pw35 had valued the house at ₹19,69,965 as on 10.3.1999 which was three months after the check period. He was unable to state the extent of construction carried out as on 31.12.1998. As against this Pw34 who is an Architect and whose services were engaged by the accused to design the said house has valued the house at ₹11,34,968. Pw34 being an Architect was visiting the house on weekly basis and as such would be in a better position to value the house as on 31.12.1998 was ₹11,34,968. Consequently, the value of the asset at serial number 8 has to be reduced by ₹8,34,997.

FDRs at the Nedungadi Bank Ltd, Cochin and FDR Number 174/97-98 at the Nedungadi Bank Ltd, Cochin

The case of the prosecution is that the accused was having ₹1,56,044 and ₹79,376 in two FDRs at the Nedungadi Bank Ltd, Cochin. The prosecution has examined Pw43 Shri PA Soma Shekar Nair. He has deposed that by application dated 8.10.1998 the accused had requested for investment of ₹75,784 in his name and in the name of Ms A Menon, by application at Exh 194 he had requested for investment of ₹75,784, by another application at Exh 195 he had requested for investment of ₹69,200 in the name of A Menon and Girija Menon and by the application at Exh 186, he requested for investment of ₹1,00,000 in account number 75/95-96. He has stated that in all six FDR receipts were issued in the name of the accused and his family. He has given details of the said FDs. He has produced the statement of account which are at Exh 197 collectively. In his cross-examination he has stated that the amount referred to in application at Exh 196 was transferred by cheque from SB Account number 4739 in the name of BR Menon and A Menon. He was unable to state as to when the said joint account was opened. He was also unable to state whether the said account was initially only in the name of A Menon and the name of BR Menon was subsequently added.

Pw43 has stated that the application at Exh 195 was signed by Mrs A Menon and G Menon. He has stated that the amount of ₹69,200 was deposited in SB Account number 4739 belonging to A Menon. He has deposed that FDRs at Exh 193 and 194 were issued from earlier amount existing in the bank in the account number 9596 in the name of BR Menon and A Menon. He has stated that the amount of ₹75,784 of FD number 176/98-98 was also from earlier existing account. He was unable to state when the said account was opened and in whose name the initial accounts were opened. He was unable to state whether the account number 4739 was initially in the name of A Menon and whether the name of accused was added in the year 1994 after the death of his father. He was also unable to state whether all six fixed deposits were made from existing accounts in the name of A Menon.

It is to be noted that the accused has stated in his deposition that his late father was working as a sales manager of a pharmaceutical firm named John Wyeth Ltd. He has stated that his father retired in 1974 and that he had sufficient earnings and also possessed a house wherein lived till 1992. The accused has deposed that his father was having accounts in various banks in Kerala including Nedungadi Bank, Syndicate Bank, etc. He has produced the passbooks of the various accounts held by his father. He has stated that upon the death of his father his name was included as a joint holding along with his mother and in some accounts that his sister Anila was joined as an additional account holder. He stated that the amount held by his late father in various banks were also in the nature of fixed deposits and that quarterly and half yearly interest was credited in the said accounts as per the instructions. He has further stated that his parents had joint Savings Account number 5087 in State Bank of Travancore and that upon the death of his father, he was added as a joint account holder along with his mother. He has stated that FDR of ₹5,000 shown in his asset was in fact the income of his parent accrued prior to the check period. Apart from the bare denials there is no evidence on record to controvert the statements made by this witness and this being the case the amount of ₹56,044 and ₹79,376 cannot be held to be the assets of the accused and as such the asset of ₹2,35,420 has to be deducted from the asset list.

Valuation of Gold Ornaments Found in Locker Number 30 at the Nedungadi Bank Ltd, Ernakulam

The case of prosecution is that the gold ornaments value of which was about ₹3,33,583 was found in locker number 30 in the name of the accused at Nedungadi Bank Ltd, Ernakulam. Learned PP Shri J Vaz has argued that the evidence of Shri B Achutan Nair vis-a-vis the documents at Exhs 150 and 151 prove that gold ornaments worth ₹3,33,583 were found in the locker number 30 in the name of the accused at Nedungadi Bank Ltd, Ernakulam. He has argued that the documents at Exh 109 is fabricated and is an afterthought. Learned PP Shri J Vaz has further argued that the said documents clearly indicates that all the items except items at serial number 1 and 22 found in the said locker were new and were unused. Learned PP Shri J Vaz contends that the prosecution has proved that the accused was holding gold ornaments worth ₹3,33,583. Learned Advocate Shri JP D'Souza has argued that the evidence of Pw19 AP Khathria clearly indicates that the gold ornaments were more than 28 years old and this corroborates the contention of the accused that the gold ornaments are part of *'Streedhan'* of Promila Menon.

It may be mentioned here that the prosecution has examined Pw28 V Achutan Nair. He has deposed that on 9.3.1999, he was requested to act as an appraiser in respect of opening of the seal of the locker number 30 in the Nedungadi Bank Ltd, Ernakulam. He has stated that the same was opened by CBI Officers and some gold ornaments were found in the said locker. He has produced memorandum, along with the list of the gold ornaments found in the locker. The said memorandum and the list is at Exh 151. He has stated that the total value of the gold ornaments and other articles found in the locker was ₹3,33,583. In his cross-examination he has stated that he is unable to state the age of the said gold ornaments. He has stated that some of these articles were very old. He was unable to say that the said gold ornaments were more than 15 years old.

It may be mentioned here that the accused has admitted that the gold ornaments found in the locker number 30 belongs to his wife. In this deposition, he has stated that the said gold ornaments were *'Streedhan'* of his wife given to her at the time of her marriage in the year 1971. It is to be noted that Pw19 AP Khathria, Under-Secretary (Vigilance), has stated in his cross-examination that the ornaments which are listed in statement number 3 collectively were shown to have been held by Mrs Promila Menon for about 28 years. The weight of the said gold ornaments was about 361.39 grams. The evidence of this witness clearly indicates that the wife of the accused possessed some gold ornaments much prior to the check period. The prosecution has not adduced any evidence to prove that the list at Exh 109 is fabricated. There is also no evidence to show as to which of these gold ornaments listed in Exh 109 or in Exh 151 were acquired during the check period. In the absence of such evidence, the gold ornaments valued at ₹3,33,586 cannot be considered as the asset acquired during check period.

17

Acquittal Judgement

Quoting from the Judgement

"The income of the accused during the check period was ₹80,51,319.58 whereas the total expenditure of the accused during the check period was ₹16,47,156.30 and the value of the assets is ₹54,58,886.53. Thus the total expenditure and assets works out to ₹71,06,042.83 which is less than the total income of the accused during the check period. This being the case, in my considered view, the prosecution has failed to establish beyond reasonable doubt that during the check period from 1.1.1991 to 31.12.1998, the accused had amassed assets disproportionate to his known lawful sources of income and thereby committed offence under Section 13(1)(e) punishable under Section 13 (2) of the Prevention of corruption Act, 1998. Hence the accused is entitled for an acquittal.

Under the circumstances and in view of the discussion supra, I pass the following:

ORDER

The accused is acquitted in respect of offence under Section 13(1)(e) punishable under Section 13(2) of the Prevention of Corruption Act, 1998.

The bail bonds stands discharged.

Documents at serial numbers 42 to 46, 51, 57 to 59, 74, 75 and 78 listed in the list of documents be returned to the accused, after the appeal period. The other documents listed in the list of documents and which are not exhibited be returned to the Investigating Officer after the appeal period.

Margoa	(Anuja Prabhudesai)"
Dated: 30.04.2012	Special Judge
	South Goa
	Margoa

The chargesheet issued on 05.11.2000 and judgement passed on 30.04.2012 will reflect the devious methods by which CBI hooked me for 13 long years ruining my retirement life. The CBI never went on an appeal, after receiving the acquittal judgement, for obvious reasons.

Here I need to point out the importance of my initial letter dated 28th September 1999 to CBI Director, Chief Vigilance Commissioner etc wherein I had clearly pointed out that my excess income over assets acquired and expenditure incurred is ₹10,51,964. After 13 years of trial, the Judge has come to the same conclusion that the excess of income over assets acquired and expenditure is ₹9,45,276.75, almost exactly the same as indicated by me in my said letter. This proved beyond any shadow of doubt the dishonesty of CBI to uphold that their charge sheet served on me to save their skin was indeed correct.

When the IO Mr Mukherjee was confronted with the enclosure by my learned lawyer Advocate D'Souza during the examination in the Court, Advocate D'Souza erroneously produced a copy of my letter dated 29th September 1999, which did not have my signature. In the initial days I had taken many copies – some of which did not have my signature at the end of this huge letter of many pages and enclosures. The shrewd IO noticed the unsigned letter and turned the Court's attention to the fact that the letter produced by my lawyer was unsigned. Advocate D'Souza was stumped to say the least. I was not in the Court either. His assistant lawyer Advocate Collasso should have been more careful. The original letter was lying in their office. Thus the IO escaped the need to explain

From: Rear Admiral B.R. Menon (Retd.)
Shipyard House
Chicalim - Goa.

Ref. No.: CMD/GSL/1 28th September, 1999.

To,
The Director
CBI, Headquarters
Block III
CGO Complex
New Delhi.

Sir,

At this point of the investigation of this unfortunate case, I am grateful that the Director has kindly agreed to analyse the details given hereunder.

Enclosed are statements of income earned during the period 1.1.91 to 31.12.98, expenditure incurred during the same period and the value of my assets at cost as on 31.12.98, the summary being as under :-

Total income earned during the period 1.1.91 to 31.12.98	Rs.88,45,920/-	Expenditure incurred during the period 1.1.91 to 31.12.98	Rs.17,18,013/-
		Value of assets acquired and held as on 31.12.98 at cost	Rs.60,75,943/-
	Rs.88,45,920/-		Rs.77,93,956/-

Excess of income over assets acquired and expenditure incurred Rs.10,51,964/-

The statements enclosed were compiled by me after the investigating officer permitted partial inspection of the same details prepared by him consequent to investigations made by him. I might mention here that the cursory inspection lasted

...2.

in the Court whether or not he had indeed received this letter and investigated it. Therefore, it took that much longer and tougher for me and for my lawyer to prove each and every point highlighted in my September 1999 letter, through bringing in various relevant evidences.

18

Vengeance by the Defence Minister – Last Nail in My Coffin

Despite the Shipyard got upgraded from Schedule 'C' PSU to a Schedule 'B' PSU, solely due to my efforts and under my command, my application for upgradation of my status from the CMD of a Schedule 'C' PSU to a Schedule 'B' PSU met with tremendous opposition in the Ministry of Defence. The main reason was the apprehension in the mind of Defence Minister, Mr George Fernandes. Whenever the file used to move to him, he used to put up some awkward query and send it back. At the end he instructed that I should go through a selection process again through the Public Sector Selection Board. When all the officers and staff of GSL were upgraded automatically, the CMD had to go through a selection process again. Quite strange. It was a trick by the Defence Minister.

I went through the selection process and the file was then put up, as a matter of routine for Vigilance Clearance. Though there was no raid by CBI at that point of time in 1998, since there were so many written complaints to the Ministry and CBI against me, the Defence Minister knew that I may not get the Vigilance Clearance as per the general practice, prior to appointment. As expected and schemed by the Defence Minister, I was not vigilance cleared. May be he directly influenced it. The Naval Headquarters was extremely unhappy that I was not given clearance to become CMD of a Schedule 'B' PSU, since I was Navy's choice. Thus, I continued as the CMD of GSL – a Schedule 'B' PSU for 2 more years – in the pay scale of a Schedule 'C' PSU. Most ludicrous. For the same reason in November 1999 when my 5 years tenure was over, though Navy recommended my extension as CMD for 3 more years since age was in my favour, I was not given extension by the Ministry since I was not Vigilance cleared by CBI.

Even after my retirement, in reply to my direct appeal to the Defence Minister, I received a wishy-washy answer, saying that since I was not cleared by the Public Sector Selection Board for the post of CMD of Schedule 'B' class Shipyard, I cannot be considered for upgrading my pay. Thus, I had the misfortune to upgrade the company of which I was the CMD to a Schedule 'B' Central Public Sector status, but continued to remain in the pay scale of a Schedule 'C' PSU as its CMD for 2 years while all the officers in GSL – got the upgraded pay scale of a Schedule 'B' company. It was quite a strange government decision. My friends advised me to legally appeal in the court against the wrong decision of the government. I did not want to open up one more legal front when I was already fighting other legal battles with the CBI and the Central Government, even during my retirement – all due to my sincere efforts towards cleansing the Shipyard and bring it up to its present pristine glory.

When my brother-in-law Col Anil Nair from Delhi visited me in Goa during the period of my Chairmanship of GSL, he was aware of the internal strife in the Company. If I recall he was even witness to some of it. Much later may be in 2010 or so when he visited Goa on holiday, he happened to go in front of the GSL. In order to have a soft drink, he stopped in front of GSL in one of the shops and while having the soft drink he enquired, just as a matter of interest to the shopkeeper as to the problems and progress of GSL now. "How is it going, are there strikes, etc now", he asked in Hindi and the shopkeeper replied to him in Hindi, "there are no strikes or any such *lafda* now; many years ago all such major issues were resolved by a Chairman called Menon with his iron hands. He was a good man but very strong and nobody could buy him at any cost. During his reign the Union leaders and workers didn't gave him help and treated him so shabbily – I was witness to it – poor old chap. He suffered terribly during his time but the officers and the workers now have been immensely benefited by his honest efforts" – my brother-in-law felt extremely proud and immediately called me and narrated this dialogue to me. I was indeed happy to hear that people around still remember me for good or bad that I have done during my 5 years of trying times in GSL. That was my tryst with GSL.

During my 70th birthday which was conducted recently I had invited some of the officers of GSL. They recalled my efforts and stated how much GSL has been benefited by my efforts. Little did they all realise that after leaving the GSL, I was prosecuted mercilessly by the CBI for 13 more years before I could live with dignity and honour again in my life. That was the price I and my family had to pay for my earnest, selfless and sincere efforts, to cleanse Goa Shipyard from its misery and miserable past!

19

Return of the Native – From Goa to Kerala

Fresh from the experience of Goa Shipyard, when I returned to Kerala, I was appointed as the Chairman and Managing Director of TELK (Transformers and Electricals Limited, Kerala). Dealing with politicians I had learned by then from running the Goa Shipyard.

My appointment soon after my return to Kerala as CMD of TELK was nothing short of a miracle. My Governor in Goa was Lt-General Jacob (Retd), the former Army Commander of Eastern sector who liberated Bangladesh from the clutches of Pakistan Army in December 1971. General Jacob became fully interested in my bold fight in streamlining GSL from the clutches of the corrupted Goan politicians. He knew the truth to the core and appreciated what I did to stem the rot of GSL in particular which became an example and a lead to the industries of Goa in general. On my return to Kerala in December 1999, he was transferred as Governor of Punjab almost simultaneously. The Kerala Governor was Mr Surjit Singh Barnala then. Mr Barnala went on a home leave to Punjab and called on his Governor in Punjab who was General Jacob. On casual conversation the Kerala Governor I understand, informed the Punjab Governor that the most difficult thing to administer in Kerala were the Industries which are under the grip of undesirable Unions and local corrupt politicians. Thereupon Lt-General Jacob informed Kerala Governor "That a son of the soil (of Kerala) called Adm Menon has returned to Kerala from Goa after cleansing a giant Industry in Goa. Give him any troublesome big Industrial setup and he will sort it out for you." This was told to me by my Governor Shri Surjit Singh Barnala himself. On Shri Barnala's return to Thiruvananthapuram, he informed this matter to the Communist Chief Minister of Kerala Shri Nayanar who directed the Industries Minister Mrs Susheela Gopalan to induct me into the government and give me a big but troublesome industry. I was made thus the CMD of TELK within a month of my return to Kerala by the Nayanar government. My appointment indeed raised many eyebrows in the industrial circle of the Kerala.

20

As CMD of M/s TELK

There were tremendous amount of financial and labour issues in TELK. While handling many of them in a very transparent and democratic way I was able to win the confidence of the workers. In order to reduce overheads I decided to reduce some of the huge number of temporary staff employed. By removing the temporary staff, supply of food in the canteen got affected. The lady employees of TELK which amounted to about 100 odd personnel, never stood in the queue in the canteen. This is when, the rest of the senior most male staff and workers of TELK stood in the queue to collect their lunch. It was a strange system. The ladies directly sat on the table and were served food by the temporary staff. After the removal of temporary staff, there was no one to serve the ladies. This agitated the ladies and consequently they decided not to stand in the queue and to go and sit on the table, waiting to be served. On the first day when this happened, the Manager of canteen called me up on the intercom and said that the ladies were sitting without taking their food for past half an hour. And it was time for the next batch of workers to come for lunch in the next 15 minutes. For convenience we had staggered the timing of lunch of different groups of workers in the canteen. To avoid the clash between the hungry ladies and the others, I personally walked into the canteen and started serving myself food to the ladies. Ashamed of the fact that they made CMD serve them food, one by one they got up, went to counter collected their food came back to their place, sat and ate the food. I never expected such a favourable result instantly. As CMD, I felt extremely pleased at my own management initiative and subsequent reaction from the ladies staff of TELK.

When the Unions reported this matter to Mrs Suseela Gopalan, Minister of Industries, stating that the present CMD is harassing the workers for no rhyme or reason, the Minister turned around and asked the Union as to why did the ladies agree to do the self help if they did not want it. The Minister with socialistic tendencies should have realised the importance of reducing the overheads of a loss making company more than the CMD! But she did not.

The mid-day lunch in TELK was a big affair – a 12 course lunch served as if in a big marriage celebration. The employees paid ₹3.5 and management paid close to ₹10. With 1,000 odd employees eating lunch, the management paid huge amount of money for subsidising the lunch. With best of my persuasion as CMD, I was unable to make the workers agree to a leaner lunch with a view to reduce the expenditure. As a strategy I then decided to take a medical examination of the workers – majority of them were 40 years and above, since there was no fresh induction in TELK for the past decade. The medical examination proved that 90% of the employees were suffering from either diabetes, blood pressure or high cholesterol. I put the entire details of all the workers in notice board and arranged a family get together and make all the families of the staff see and realise the health conditions of their husbands. They were shocked to note that their husbands were patients of diseases which could impair their health drastically and reduce their life expectancy. The families requested me to do something and I said the only way I can help is to control their lunch by serving a clinical diet. They all agreed. There were 3 queues in the canteen. The BP queue, the cholesterol queue and the diabetes queue. Separate clinically permissible diet queues were thus setup. This improved the health conditions of the workers tremendously and consequently the cost of the lunch also came down drastically. However instead of realising the benefit to the company and an improved health of the workers due to my initiative, I was accused by the then Chief Minister Shri Nayanar saying that I have wilfully reduced the quality and quantum of lunch served to the employees in a very autocratic and cruel manner. Perhaps, the former CM did not realise that it was a volunteer suggestion by the families of the workers to improve the health of the workers. As CMD, I only implemented it. I also renovated the canteen, toilets, store rooms and rest rooms of the workers to that of the modern setup. I used to inspect the factory almost daily, walking around to every nook and corner and enquire with employees their wellbeing. All such actions increased the faith of workers on the CMD tremendously. The production improved. TELK received export orders from Oman for making huge transformers. In that period as CMD, I requested for substantial government loan with low interest to pay up the loan we have taken from the State Bank of Travancore (SBT) (presently merged with SBI). Without the huge loan that we had asked from the government, we would have not been able to give the necessary bank guarantee to Oman government. Since the loan was not coming through easily, I put in my resignation in a single letter without indicating any reason. That letter of mine remained in the ministry file without action. As a result Mrs Suseela Gopalan the Industries Minister realising the dire need, some amount of loan was however sanctioned by the government. With that and many other persuasions, we got the necessary bank guarantee and got the orders from the Oman. Those were executed on time, which gave great prestige to the management and staff of the TELK. Other industries in Kerala started looking up to TELK. The workers developed immense confidence in the efforts of their CMD.

Then the government changed and the Congress government headed by Shri AK Antony came into power. His Industries Minister was Mr Kunjalikutty. TELK was turning around and the Congress government had an eye on the profit making TELK and its huge area of land lying unused. The property being near the airport was a valuable asset financially for TELK. I was certainly not their choice as CMD, since it was the previous Communist government who had selected me as CMD. Perhaps the Industries Minister had also his own people lined up for the job. In that period I had to pay bonus to the workers which they had earned with their efforts. The pattern in Kerala was that the company paid bonus with the approval of Minister and Minister earned all the glory of payment of bonus. For that purpose I went to Thiruvananthapuram to meet the Minister in his office to take his permission for payment of bonus as per usual practice. The Minister Mr Kunjalikutty did not like me at all since I was not yielding to many of his demands like induction of some of his favourites into the company, promotion of some of his favourites in the company etc etc. He also did not like my straight forward and strong attitude in managing and developing TELK. He also knew that the entire staff irrespective of any political factions was supporting my administration with total transparency. To the workers of TELK this was a totally different experience. And Mr Kunjalikutty showed his aversion to me by neglecting me totally when I waited in his office for 2 days with his knowledge and knowing the purpose for which I have come. On the 3rd day when he was coming to the office I just informed him on the way that I am going to pay the workers their bonus rightfully earned by them with or without the Minister's approval. He uttered something in reply but I walked away, came to Angamali from Thiruvananthapuram and distributed the bonus to my workers. That, without Minister's approval I paid the bonus to the workers was headlines in the newspapers of the Kerala the next day. Two days later I received a letter from the government terminating my appointment, accepting my age old resignation letter which was available in the file. The Minister himself, I believe initiated this process. The spineless bureaucracy as per the direction of the Minister dugout my old resignation letter from the file and gave it to him on

TELK for sale?

a platter. A newspaper cutting of the period with a caption "TELK for sale?".

It was a very vengeful act by Shri Kunjalikutty. He found in me a competent, honest and an efficient CMD but will not yield to the whims and fancies of the minister. The workers of TELK stopped working in protest against my removal. Upon request from the government, I requested the Unions and the workers to continue their good work without risking further loss to the company for my sake. They resumed to work in right earnest thereafter.

The above was one of the nasty interventions by the government of Kerala in running of a profitably running Industry with a strong CMD as its head. That I had fought with the Congress ministry in power, gave me a stamp as that of astute Communist. After 5

Rear Admiral B.R. Menon Appointed Advisor To Govt. Of Kerala

Rear Admiral B.R. Menon V.S.M (Retd.) former Chairman and MD of Goa shipyard Ltd. Goa and Transformers and Electricals Ltd. (TELK) at Angamally, Kerala has been appointed as ADVISOR to the Govt. of Kerala.

A very active Fellow of the Kochi Chapter of Institute of Marine Engineers (India) Ltd, Admiral Menon will advise the Kerala Govt. on speedy development of Inland Waterways and modernization of all minor ports in Kerala.

A Marine Engineer of outstanding professional standing, Admiral Menon has contributed hugely in development of the Naval Repair facilities at the Naval Base in Kochi in the development of the Ultra modern Technology repair base of the Navy at KARWAR, and also as the Director of Marine Engineering at NHQ, New Delhi during the collapse of the Soviet Union.

Presently Admiral Menon is Advisor Emeritus with the Cochin University of Science and Technology, in the department of Marine Engineering and Ship building. ■

Marine Engineers Review (India) *December 2006* www.imare.in 35

years, when the Congress government was voted out and a Communist government under the leadership of Shri Achuthanandan as the Chief Minister of Kerala came to power, I was handpicked by the Communist government as their Advisor for Development of Inland Waterways and Minor Ports of Kerala.

21

As Advisor to the Government of Kerala

Initially it was a pleasure working with Shri Achuthanandan who is considered as the Fidel Castro of Kerala. I worked as dedicatedly as I could to improve the Inland Waterways and the Minor Ports of Kerala. The NW III (National Waterways III) was being developed by the Central Government from Kollam to Kottapuram – a distance of 257 km. But due to many hurdles such as objections from the local peoples on building bank protection, dredging and removal of dredged materials, deepening of the Waterways to 2.5 m depth, acquiring land for widening of the Waterways to a width of 32 m – all these necessary activities to develop the Waterways met with great objections from the local people. When I took over as the Advisor, the NW III development in Kerala was on a stand still. Slowly but surely I involved with the local people by interacting with them very closely and got them to agree to the various developmental requirements of NW III. What could not be done for the past decade by the Central Government was achieved now within a span of 12 months as a result of my direct involvement. This resulted in my getting tremendous recognition in the eyes of the officers of the Central Government. The Chief Minister Mr Achuthanandan was mighty pleased with my performance. Simultaneously, I also advised in developments of state waterways which were not connected to NW III. There are 44 west flowing rivers in Kerala; most of them were navigable in the olden days. Those were all developed by the colonial powers – the Portuguese, the Dutch and the British. But due to disuse they all got clogged, silted and blocked. One by one I got them navigable in small stretches first. To connect Kollam to Thiruvananthapuram, the biggest hurdles were the twin tunnels at Varkala. These subterranean water tunnels made by British in 1862 or thereabouts primarily to connect, Kollam to the Southern cities of Kerala like Trivandrum and Vizhinjam. I decided to take the CM Mr Achuthanandan through the Varkala tunnel to examine the present condition and also to give a momentum to the development of waterways in Kerala in the eyes of the public. But the security staff objected to it by stating that, "It is unsafe for the CM to travel" since it was lying unused for at least 4 to 5 decades – nearly after our Independence. I therefore decided to take a trip through the tunnel as a guinea pig. I took a trip – may be the first trip by anyone after 50 years – through the twin tunnels of Varkala, examined the existing structures and reported the matter to the CM. Mr Achuthanandan was very pleased and agreed to come with me to observe the internals of the tunnel. Thus I had the fortune to accompany the CM and we took a trip through the tunnel which was considered a very positive bold step taken by the government for the development of internal waterways of Kerala. All these and many more of my involved activities such as removal of fishing nets from the waterways – Chinese nets and single pole nets – which got removed by persuasion, financial help and other means. Also I was able to get substantial funds from the Central Government for the development of minor ports of Kerala by explaining in person to Mr Montek Singh Ahluwalia, the then Deputy Chairman of Planning Commission, the dire need of development of the minor ports of Kerala which alone will, I convinced him, improve financial conditions of the people who lived in the coastal areas in the Kerala. When funds started flowing, Mr Achuthanandan started publicly praising me. This caused many eyebrows to raise and the faction in the Communist government which were against the CM started plotting against me. The various contractors who were involved in developing the waterways could also not suffer me either any longer since they could not buy me nor could they do a poor quality work when I was supervising and managing the work. This hurt their profit margin heavily. Thus with the help of the anti-CM faction in the Communist party and with the help of the disgruntled contractors, they hatched a plan to trap me. The details of the scheme that they had planned and meticulously executed were as follows.

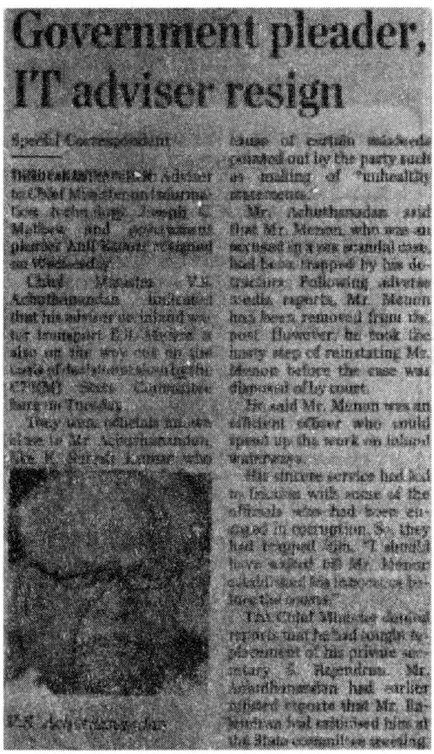

Government pleader, IT adviser resign

[illegible]

... because of certain misdeeds pointed out by the party such as making of "unhealthy statements."

Mr. Achuthanandan said that Mr. Menon, who was accused in a sex scandal case, had been trapped by his detractors. Following adverse media reports, Mr. Menon has been removed from the post. However, he took the hasty step of reinstating Mr. Menon before the case was disposed of by court.

He said Mr. Menon was an efficient officer who could speed up the work on inland waterways.

His sincere service had led to frictions with some of the officials who had been engaged in corruption. So, they had trapped him. "I should have waited till Mr. Menon established his innocence before the courts."

The Chief Minister denied reports that he had sought replacement of his private secretary [illegible] Mr. Achuthanandan had earlier [illegible] reports that Mr. [illegible] had [illegible] him at the State committee meeting.

22

Government Servant Trapped – Price Paid for Honesty

On a call from the CM's PS Mrs Sheela Thomas IAS, I took the early morning train from Kochi and reached Thiruvananthapuram government guest house at about 11.15 AM since I was to meet the CM in the Niyamasabha (Legislative Assembly) at about 12 AM. At about 11.30 AM I had a knock on my door and I found one of my old maids who was working with us in Kochi 3 years ago came into the room on the plea that she wanted some financial help for sending her children to school. On asking as to how she found out that I was in Thiruvananthapuram she said that she contacted to my home at Kochi and come to know of it. It was a lie which we came to know later. Within 5 minutes of her arrival, a set of police team including some lady police headed by the Circle Inspector of

Police came into my room. They then asked the maid why she is here and then she immediately lied and said that I had called her. She further stated that she has come to the room as per my direction to satisfy me in whatever means. Then the police searched her body and realised ₹ 10,000. She then told the police that this money was given by me. I knew then that it was a well-planned trap both by the home department and the guest house people. Within next 5 minutes to my great surprise, I saw the reps of all the TV channels and media in front of my rooms taking photographs. Surprisingly within 15 minutes that is by 12 o'clock, the entire TV channels were beaming this news to the surprise of many including that of the CM who was waiting for me in the Legislative Assembly hall. The police had removed my mobile phone to prevent me from contacting anybody. I was arrested as per the immoral criminal procedure and let out on bail. My maid also was arrested and let out on bail by me. I stood the financial guarantee for her also. We were medically examined and it was proved that the maid did not have evidence of any sexual intercourse during the past 72 hours. I came to know much later during the investigation period that she has been advised by the contractors to say so and the money was given to her by them so that she must act as per their advice and to tell the police that I had given the amount.

But all that was after the incident. The newspapers and the channels worked as usual with utmost urgency when they got such juicy news and spread it world over. My image and reputation were damaged irreparably. The CM was forced to remove me immediately from the post which is what the corrupt contractors and the faction of the CM's opposite group wanted. However couple of days later the CM called me and told me that he knew it is a trap since his PS had called him after talking to me around 11.30 AM confirming that I had arrived and that I will meet the CM at 12 o'clock as per schedule. Therefore it was next to impossible that I would plan and indulge in such an activity just before meeting the CM. But the damage has already done and that he was forced to remove me from the post prior to any deep investigation.

Back in Kochi I engaged a reputed lawyer who heard my stories and took up a case against the police department and State administration. My lawyer's plea to the High Court at Kochi was just recalling the timings of the event with evidence, that is my arrival in the guest house at 11.30 AM, the maid coming to the reception of guest house at 11.31 AM enquiring which room I am staying and she reaching the room at 11.32 AM and at 11.35 the woman police and the other police arrive in my room and see both of us in fully dressed condition. I am sitting in the chair and she is standing. Who informed the police to come and why?

At 11.45 AM the reps of media and TV channels arrived and taken photographs and in an extremely swift move, they managed to send the photos to the channels which beamed it at 12 AM? Who directed them to do such exceptionally efficient job? How did they come into the guest house in the first place? Who informed the media and the TV channels? And finally my lawyer argued in the court, where was the time in the given scenario for them to indulge in any activities as alleged? He further argued that the medical report of the maid proved negative.

The prosecution case was dismissed in the first sitting itself with strictures against the government and the police department for unwanted hasty action without proper investigation and before filing a chargesheet. It was proved conclusively that it was a trap setup by the people who are against me and to the ruling faction of the Communist government. I was exonerated within 2 months of my dismissal from the post.

Thereupon the Chief Minister requested me to join back as his Advisor in the government immediately. First I refused since I felt as a CM he could have done much more to relieve me from the prosecution before the police filing the chargesheet against me. But he did not. Perhaps he did not want to get involved into this nasty case. But later when he knew that it was a trap and when I was exonerated, he wanted me

THE HINDU • WEDNESDAY, MARCH 17, 2010

Official laxity delaying waterways project: VS

Says work on the project progressing now

Special Correspondent

- Says sanction accorded to 120 projects
- 'Officials interested only in selling sand'

THIRUVANANTHAPURAM: Bureaucratic laxity is delaying the completion of inland waterways development project in the State, Chief Minister V.S. Achuthanandan has said.

To questions in the Assembly on Tuesday, the Chief Minister said the Twelfth Finance Commission had awarded Rs.56.22 crore for the project during 2006-07 and Rs.151.98 crore during 2007-10. Administrative sanction was accorded for 120 projects during 2006-07 of which 79 had been completed.

Out of the 127 works taken up during 2007-10, 25 had been completed. Officials were interested only in making money by selling sand and were not keen on completing the project. When his adviser to Inland Waterways Development B.R. Menon took action against erring officials, there was an attempt to tarnish his image and was allegedly trapped in a sex scandal case. Later, the High Court acquitted him and had been reinstated. Now, work on the project was progressing, but was unable to complete it within the month-end, he said.

Forest Minister Benny Vis-

to join back immediately. Though I was hesitant in the beginning, my friends advised me that by joining back in the same post alone will help to remove the stain and black mark on my reputation. So I joined back as the Advisor to the government and worked for another 2 years. It was the most harrowing part of my term in the Communist government (CPM) of Kerala. One thing was clear. When you cry, you cry alone; there is no one to help you. CPM government was the last one to boldly come out and help.

When the government changed again, Mr Oommen Chandy the Congress CM wanted me to continue as his Advisor but some other ministers in his cabinet including my old friend Mr Kunjalikutty advised him against taking me as new Congress government's Advisor, since they felt I might leak informations to the Communist group who are in the opposition. My term thus ended there.

23
Epilogue

To draw a humane portrait of the 'victim', who also happens to be the author of a kind of autobiographical narration of victim's life experiences while valiantly fighting corruption and corrupt practices in public institutions, is not easy. The attempt has been of course to move the consciousness of the country, stir the hearts of hundreds of readers of the book and create an unforgettable moment in time, a drumbeat of the 'honest victim' without being idolatrous. Whether it is in my desperate but bold attempts for five years to cleanse Goa Shipyard from its miserable past, stop it's corrupt time honoured practices, rejuvenate and drag the Yard on to a delineated well groomed path of professional excellence or whether to improve the efficacy and functioning of government body in Kerala towards cleansing it's deep rooted unethical practices with a view to developing the Inland Waterways of Kerala – that too working directly under the Chief Minister – the ingrained politics seethed in corrupt practices with the sole aim of making a "quick dirty buck" stood in the way of my attempts to cleanse the system. And when a gallant soldier fights regardless of the hurdles thrown at him with a "never say die attitude", the machinery supporting the corrupt makes the gallant soldier ineffective and worthless by hooking him up through CBI orchestrated cases or through other legal entanglements. Both in Goa Shipyard and as the Advisor to Kerala, I met with exactly same kind of style and disgraceful behaviour and responses from the highest Central and State machinery – but at varying intensities. In both cases, the aim of the corrupt ruling machinery are the same; by whatever means nothing should stop the "flow of ill-gotten funds" to them. The end justifies the means. There is nothing like just and honest practices in civil life, as rule. Honesty is at public auction for the best bidder, the victim's misery and untold sufferings, notwithstanding. The valiant fight to cleanse and improve the system by a few fools is nothing but a minor thorn strewn on their march towards devour the ill-gotten National wealth. That minor thorns will be removed at any cost with the scant neglect it deserves! That is the working norm generally seen in our country, unfortunately.

In our way through life, the strength of our character will often be tested at every stage of our professional and social life – tested by fellow human beings who believe that conscience and conviction can at times be sacrificed for material benefits. It is here that you will have your greatest battle; for once you sacrifice a principle against better judgment, you have not only compromised yourself in the eyes of your fellow human beings but you have fooled yourself, which is, perhaps, the worst thing you can do in life.

An officer's physical and moral courage and immaculate integrity was not as much the need of the hour during the earlier times, as much as it is nowadays. In today's world of slipping ethical standards, the hallmark qualities which once traditionally defined the military and civilian ethos, have slowly begun to erode and wane.

The bounden responsibility of our National leaders is to toughen the character of ordinary young men and women – the leaders of our Nation tomorrow – and to transform and mould them to resist unflinchingly the sacrifice of the conscience and conviction when put to test by fellow human beings. One has to lead by example. It is the only style of leadership that ultimately counts.

A leader's strength of character, his moral compass, his compassion, his selflessness, his insistence on leading by example, his unquestionable personal probity, all are commonly needed attributes, not only in the profession of arms, but especially in the senior echelons of Corporations, Bureaucracy and Governance itself. That is what a CEO ought to be in our country today. Only then there will be a ray of hope of resurrection of our Nation from where we are today.

> "Educating the mind without educating the heart is no education at all." – Aristotle

Bharat Mata Ki Jai.

Index